Soft Skills Mastering

Essentials of Professional and Personal Success in Today's World

David A. Cohen

Table of Contents

Chapter One: Introduction and Key Concepts

Today, the term "soft skills" has burgeoned beyond its traditional confines, evolving into a critical set of competencies that dictate the success of individuals in both their professional and personal spheres. Unlike hard skills, which are measurable and often specific to a certain type of task or activity, soft skills encompass the subtler, more nuanced aspects of human behavior and interaction. These are the skills that enable us to navigate the complexities of social interactions, build and maintain relationships, and effectively communicate and collaborate with others.

The modern context has amplified the importance of soft skills, as the global economy and the nature of work itself have undergone significant transformations. The rise of digital communication platforms, the shift toward team-based work in diverse and often remote settings, and the increasing pace of change all demand a high degree of adaptability, emotional intelligence, and interpersonal skills. In this era, the ability to work well with others, manage one's emotions and reactions, think critically and solve problems creatively, and communicate effectively across a range of mediums is just as crucial—if not more so—than technical expertise or academic knowledge.

Moreover, the definition of soft skills in today's world extends to cultural competency and global awareness, reflecting the interconnected nature of our societies and economies. The ability to understand, respect, and work effectively with individuals from a wide array of cultural backgrounds is a vital component of soft skills. This encompasses not only language and communication style but also an appreciation for different perspectives and practices.

In defining soft skills within the modern context, it's also essential to consider the role of emotional intelligence. This involves more than just understanding one's own emotions; it's about empathizing with others, navigating social nuances, and making decisions that account for emotional and human factors. Emotional intelligence underpins many other soft skills, serving as a foundation for effective leadership, teamwork, and interpersonal relations.

The importance of soft skills today cannot be overstated. They are often the distinguishing factor in employment decisions, career advancement, and professional success. Employers increasingly recognize that while technical skills may get someone in the door, it's their soft skills that contribute most significantly to their performance, the quality of their work, and their ability to lead and inspire others. Consequently, the modern workforce demands individuals who are not only proficient in their technical fields but also adept at managing relationships, understanding and leveraging emotional dynamics, and adapting to rapidly changing environments.

Soft Skills in Professional and Personal Growth

As the fabric of workplaces and the dynamics of personal life evolve, soft skills have emerged as essential tools for navigating the complexities of both realms.

In the realm of professional development, soft skills such as communication, teamwork, emotional intelligence, and adaptability are increasingly recognized as critical determinants of success. The modern workplace demands not only technical proficiency but also the ability to collaborate effectively, resolve conflicts, and lead with empathy. These competencies enable individuals to build strong relationships with colleagues, manage diverse teams, and navigate the complexities of global and culturally diverse work environments. As industries continue to evolve with technological advancements, the ability to learn and adapt has become crucial. Soft skills facilitate this by fostering a mindset open to growth and learning, enabling professionals to stay relevant in their fields.

The impact of soft skills extends beyond the professional sphere into personal growth and development. Skills such as emotional regulation, empathy, and effective communication are foundational to building and maintaining healthy relationships. They enhance one's ability to understand and connect with others, fostering a sense of community and belonging. Furthermore, soft skills such as resilience, stress management, and adaptability are vital for navigating life's challenges. They contribute to a person's overall well-being and happiness, equipping them to handle the uncertainties and pressures of daily life.

The interplay between soft skills in professional and personal contexts is also significant. The competencies developed in one area invariably enrich the other. For instance, effective communication and teamwork in the workplace can improve interpersonal relationships at home and in social settings. Similarly, emotional intelligence gained through personal experiences can enhance professional interactions and leadership abilities. This synergy underscores the holistic value of soft skills, highlighting their role in achieving a balanced and fulfilling life.

The Evolution of Soft Skills in the Workplace and Society

Historically, the industrial age placed a premium on hard skills, with success in the workplace largely measured by technical proficiency and productivity. In this era, the emphasis was on tangible outputs and efficiency, with less regard for the interpersonal dynamics or emotional intelligence that lay beneath the surface of work processes. However, as the economy transitioned from industrial manufacturing to service-oriented and knowledge-based sectors, the landscape of work underwent a profound transformation. This shift heralded the rise of soft skills as critical components of professional success.

The advent of the information age and the digital revolution further accelerated this shift, placing a greater emphasis on communication, collaboration, and adaptability. The workplace became increasingly globalized and interconnected, demanding a new set of skills that transcended traditional boundaries and disciplines. In this context, the ability to work effectively in diverse teams, communicate across cultural divides, and adapt to rapidly changing technologies became just as important as technical expertise.

The evolution of soft skills in the workplace mirrored broader societal changes, where values such as empathy, inclusivity, and emotional well-being gained prominence. The growing recognition of mental health as a critical component of overall health, along with an increasing awareness of social justice issues, has emphasized the importance of developing a more holistic set of skills that cater to the human aspects of work and life. This has led to a greater appreciation of skills such as emotional intelligence, resilience, and ethical leadership, which are now seen as indispensable to navigating the complexities of modern society.

Today, the narrative around soft skills has evolved to reflect a more integrated view of professional and personal success. They are not seen merely as a set of complementary skills but as foundational to achieving a balanced and fulfilling life. The contemporary workplace values individuals who can lead with compassion, innovate through collaboration, and adapt to the unforeseen with agility. Similarly, society at large benefits from individuals who are emotionally intelligent, socially responsible, and committed to lifelong learning.

Chapter Two: Communication Mastery

Verbal Communication: Techniques and Best Practices

Verbal communication stands at the core of human interaction, enabling us to express ideas, convey emotions, and foster connections. It encompasses not only the words we choose but also how we say them—tone, pace, and clarity. In the realm of professional and personal growth, mastering verbal communication is indispensable.

Clarity and Conciseness

In an era where attention spans are short and information overload is a common challenge, the ability to articulate your thoughts in a clear and concise manner stands out as a crucial skill. Clear communication ensures that your message is understood without the need for repetitive clarification, while conciseness respects the listener's or reader's time, focusing on delivering maximum value with minimum verbosity. This skill is especially valuable in professional settings, educational environments, and even in personal relationships, where effective communication can significantly impact outcomes.

Strategies for Achieving Clarity and Conciseness

- **Preparation**: Spend time organizing your thoughts before you communicate. This includes identifying the key points you want to make and the most straightforward way to present them.

- **Simplicity**: Use simple language and avoid jargon or technical terms unless you are certain your audience understands them. Complex language can alienate or confuse listeners.

- **Focus**: Stay on topic and avoid digressing into unrelated subjects. Keep your message focused on the primary objective.

- **Brevity**: Practice saying what you need to say in fewer words. Challenge yourself to eliminate filler words and redundant expressions that do not add value to your message.

Before you begin to speak or write, take a moment to clearly define the purpose of your communication. What is the core message you need to convey? Who is your audience, and what is the most effective way to reach them? By answering these questions, you can structure your communication more effectively, ensuring that your message is both clear and concise.

Tone of Voice

The tone of voice plays a critical role in how your message is perceived. It's not just about what you say, but how you say it. Your tone can convey enthusiasm, sincerity, concern, or confidence, which can significantly affect the listener's engagement and reaction. Conversely, a negative tone, such as sounding bored, irritated, or condescending, can alienate your audience, leading to resistance or misunderstanding.

Adapting Your Tone

- **Audience Awareness**: Tailor your tone to your audience. A professional, formal tone may be appropriate for a business meeting, while a more relaxed, informal tone might be better suited for a casual conversation.

- **Emotional Intelligence**: Be attuned to the emotional state of your audience and the context of the conversation. Adjusting your tone to show empathy, respect, or excitement can enhance the connection with your audience.

- **Consistency**: While adapting your tone to different situations, ensure that it aligns with your overall message and personal or brand identity. Consistency helps in building trust and credibility.

Reflect on the emotional outcome you desire from your communication. Do you want to inspire confidence, elicit sympathy, or motivate action? Consider the context and your relationship with the audience to choose an appropriate tone. Practicing mindfulness and emotional intelligence can help you adjust your tone intuitively to suit the situation and achieve the desired effect.

Active Listening

Active listening is an essential component of effective communication. It involves giving full attention to the speaker, understanding their message, responding appropriately, and remembering what was said. This process not only aids in better understanding but also shows respect and appreciation for the speaker's perspective. Active listening can prevent miscommunications, resolve conflicts, and build stronger relationships.

Techniques for Active Listening

- **Engagement**: Use non-verbal cues, such as nodding or maintaining eye contact, to show you are engaged.

- **Feedback**: Provide feedback by summarizing or asking questions to confirm understanding. This encourages open dialogue and clarifies any ambiguities.

- **Empathy**: Try to understand the speaker's perspective and feelings. Empathetic listening can bridge gaps in communication and foster stronger connections.

Focus on being present in the conversation, setting aside distractions and preconceived notions. Approach each conversation with the intent to understand fully rather than respond. Encourage the speaker with verbal affirmations and open-ended questions that prompt further explanation. This level of engagement demonstrates respect for the speaker and can lead to more productive and meaningful conversations.

Feedback

Feedback is a cornerstone of effective communication and personal development. It allows individuals and organizations to grow by identifying strengths and highlighting areas for improvement. Constructive feedback, when delivered properly, can motivate individuals, enhance performance, and strengthen relationships. It provides a foundation for learning and development, offering clear guidance on how behaviors or performance can be improved.

Strategies for Delivering Constructive Feedback

- **Specificity**: Be specific about what actions or behaviors are being addressed. Vague feedback can be confusing and unhelpful.

- **Timeliness**: Offer feedback as close to the event as possible to ensure relevance and clarity.

- **Empathy**: Deliver feedback with empathy and understanding. Acknowledge the individual's efforts and perspectives to ensure the feedback is received in a constructive manner.

- **Focus on Improvement**: Emphasize solutions and opportunities for growth rather than dwelling solely on the negatives.

The "sandwich" method is a popular technique for providing feedback. This method involves starting with positive feedback (something the individual does well), followed by constructive criticism (areas for improvement), and concluding with additional positive reinforcement. This technique can help soften the impact of critical feedback and encourage a more receptive and positive response. However, it's important to ensure that the positive aspects are genuine and relevant, not just filler to cushion the criticism.

Adaptability

Adaptability in communication involves adjusting your message, language, tone, and body language to better suit the context of the conversation and the audience. This flexibility can greatly enhance the effectiveness of your communication, making it possible to connect with a wide range of individuals across different situations. Adaptability is particularly important in multicultural environments, where understanding and respecting cultural differences can improve communication and relationships.

How to Improve Communication Adaptability

- **Cultural Awareness**: Educate yourself about the cultural backgrounds and communication styles of your audience. This knowledge can guide you in choosing the most appropriate language, tone, and gestures.

- **Active Listening**: Use active listening to pick up cues about the audience's response to your communication style and adjust accordingly.

- **Feedback**: Seek and be open to feedback about how your communication is received. This can offer insights into how you might need to adapt in different contexts.

To improve adaptability, cultivate a mindset of learning and curiosity about the people you interact with. Observe and ask questions to understand their communication preferences and needs. Be willing to step outside your comfort zone and experiment with different communication styles. This approach can help you become more versatile and effective in your interactions.

Practice and Reflection

Verbal communication is a skill that benefits greatly from continuous practice and thoughtful reflection. Engaging regularly in diverse communication settings—from informal conversations to formal presentations—provides valuable experience. Reflecting on these experiences helps to consolidate learning, recognize patterns, and identify areas for improvement.

Approaches to Practice and Reflection

- **Diverse Opportunities**: Seek out varied opportunities for speaking, such as joining a debate club, participating in workshops, or volunteering for presentations.

- **Self-Evaluation**: After each communication event, take time to reflect on what went well and what could be improved. Consider aspects like clarity, tone, engagement, and listener response.

- **Feedback Loop**: Incorporate feedback from others into your reflection process. Constructive criticism from peers, mentors, or audiences can provide objective insights.

Set specific, achievable goals for your verbal communication skills. For instance, you might aim to improve your storytelling abilities, enhance your persuasive speaking, or become more effective at active listening. Use each speaking opportunity as a chance to work on these goals, and reflect afterward on your progress. Seeking feedback from trusted individuals who can provide honest, constructive insights will further enhance your learning and growth in verbal communication.

Non-Verbal Communication: Using Body Language Effectively

Non-verbal communication, or the subtle art of conveying messages without words, plays a critical role in human interaction. It encompasses facial expressions, body movements, gestures, posture, eye contact, and even the use of space. Despite its silent nature, non-verbal cues can communicate volumes, often speaking louder than words.

Facial Expressions

Facial expressions are a universal language, capable of conveying emotions and reactions across cultural boundaries. They can express a wide range of feelings, from joy, surprise, and trust to anger, disgust, and confusion, often without a single word being spoken. This ability to communicate emotions quickly and effectively makes facial expressions a critical component of interpersonal communication.

Interpreting and Using Facial Expressions

- **Empathy and Connection**: Recognizing and responding to the facial expressions of others can facilitate empathy and emotional connection. It allows communicators to adjust their message and approach based on the visual feedback they receive.

- **Consistency**: Ensuring that your facial expressions align with your verbal messages is crucial. Inconsistencies can lead to confusion or mistrust, while congruence enhances the credibility and effectiveness of your communication.

- **Cultural Sensitivity**: While many facial expressions are universal, cultural differences can influence their interpretation. Being aware of these nuances is important in multicultural interactions.

Actively practice recognizing and understanding the facial expressions of those around you. This can improve your ability to interpret non-verbal cues accurately. Additionally, strive to ensure that your own facial expressions are genuine and match the message you intend to convey. A sincere smile, for instance, can greatly enhance communication by making you appear more approachable and empathetic.

Gestures and Body Movements

Gestures are a dynamic component of communication that can reinforce, complement, or even replace verbal messages. They can add emphasis to speech, illustrate concepts visually, and express emotions or attitudes.

Understanding how to use gestures effectively can make communication more engaging and clearer.

Strategies for Effective Use of Gestures

- **Clarity and Emphasis**: Use gestures deliberately to clarify or emphasize key points in your communication. For example, a pointed finger can direct attention, while a thumbs-up can affirm a positive message.

- **Cultural Awareness**: Gestures can have very different meanings in different cultures. What is considered a positive gesture in one culture may be offensive in another. Always be mindful of the cultural context of your audience when using gestures.

- **Consistency**: Ensure your gestures align with your verbal messages. Inconsistent or contradictory signals can confuse your audience.

Incorporate open and welcoming gestures into your communication to enhance your message and encourage positive interactions. Practice being mindful of your body language in various settings to become more aware of how your gestures affect your communication. Adjust your body language to be appropriate for the context and the audience, ensuring that it supports and reinforces your verbal messages.

Posture

Posture goes beyond mere physical stance; it communicates attitudes, feelings, and levels of engagement. An open, upright posture can project confidence and openness to dialogue, making it a vital aspect of effective communication, especially in face-to-face interactions.

Influencing Perceptions with Posture

- **Confidence and Approachability**: An upright, relaxed posture not only makes you appear more confident but also more approachable, facilitating easier communication.

- **Engagement and Interest**: Leaning slightly forward can demonstrate interest and engagement, encouraging others to communicate openly in return.

- **Receptiveness**: Maintaining an open posture, without crossing arms or legs, signals receptiveness to the speaker's ideas, fostering a more collaborative and positive communication environment.

Be conscious of your posture during interactions. Adopting a posture that signals engagement and openness can significantly impact the dynamics of the conversation. When listening, show your attentiveness through your posture. When speaking, use your stance to convey confidence and openness. Regularly practicing good posture can also improve your physical well-being, which, in turn, positively affects your ability to communicate effectively.

Eye Contact

Eye contact is a critical element of effective communication, serving as a non-verbal cue that can significantly influence the dynamics of interpersonal interactions. It plays a key role in conveying interest, attention, and confidence. Eye contact can also be a tool for assessing the other person's reactions and feelings. However, the appropriateness of eye contact varies significantly across cultures, making it a nuanced aspect of communication.

Cultural Considerations and Best Practices

- **Cultural Variability**: In some cultures, direct eye contact is seen as a sign of respect and attentiveness, while in others, it may be perceived as challenging or disrespectful. Understanding these cultural nuances is crucial in international or multicultural settings.

- **Balancing Eye Contact**: Finding the right balance of eye contact is essential. Too much can be intimidating or confrontational, while too little can be perceived as disinterest or lack of confidence.

- **Contextual Sensitivity**: The context of the interaction—whether it's a formal business meeting or a casual conversation—also influences the appropriate level of eye contact.

Strive to maintain eye contact that feels natural and appropriate for the situation and cultural context. Use eye contact to show you are engaged and listening, but be mindful not to stare or make the other person uncomfortable. Adjusting your level of eye contact to match the norms of your audience can create a stronger connection and facilitate trust.

Proxemics: The Use of Space

Proxemics refers to the study of how people use space in communication and how various differences in that use can affect interactions. The distance you maintain from others during an interaction can convey a range of messages, from intimacy and familiarity to formality and detachment. This aspect of non-verbal communication can greatly impact the perception of social and personal relationships.

Navigating Spatial Dynamics

- **Personal Space**: Different cultures have different norms regarding personal space. Being too close can be seen as intrusive in some cultures, while standing too far away might be perceived as aloof or disinterested in others.

- **Adapting to Context**: The appropriate use of space varies depending on the context of the communication, such as the setting (public vs. private), the relationship between the individuals, and the nature of the conversation.

Be observant and sensitive to the comfort levels of those you are interacting with, adjusting your physical distance accordingly. When in doubt, err on the side of giving more space, and let the other person close the distance if they choose. Understanding and respecting personal and cultural boundaries regarding space can significantly enhance communication effectiveness.

Synchrony: Mirroring and Matching

Synchrony, or the mirroring of non-verbal cues such as posture, gestures, and facial expressions, is a subtle yet powerful way to build rapport and show empathy in communication. This mimicry, when done naturally, can signal agreement and affinity without words, fostering a sense of connection and understanding.

Practicing Synchrony Effectively

- **Subtle Mirroring**: The key to effective synchrony is subtlety. Mirroring should not be overt or mimicry; instead, it should be a natural reflection of the other person's body language.

- **Building Rapport**: Matching the tone of voice, pace of speech, and body language of your conversation partner can make them feel more understood and connected to you.

- **Awareness and Sensitivity**: Be mindful of the other person's reactions to ensure your attempts at synchrony are being received positively. Misinterpretation or overuse of mirroring techniques can lead to discomfort or perceived insincerity.

Practice attentive observation of the non-verbal cues of those you interact with and gently incorporate aspects of their body language into your own. This process should be gradual and respectful, aiming to enhance communication rather than mimic. Being genuinely interested in and attentive to the conversation will often naturally lead to synchrony, enhancing the communication experience for both parties.

Digital Communication: Navigating Online Interactions and Etiquette

In the digital age, communication transcends physical boundaries, connecting us across the globe through emails, social media, instant messaging, and video calls. While digital communication offers unprecedented convenience and speed, it also presents unique challenges and nuances.

Professionalism in digital communication is critical for maintaining a positive and respectful professional image. The way you communicate electronically can significantly impact your relationships with colleagues, clients, and other professionals. Professional digital interactions should mirror the decorum and respect you would show in in-person encounters.

Guidelines for Professional Digital Communication

- **Formality**: Use a formal tone in initial communications or with individuals you do not know well. You can adjust the level of formality based on the response and your relationship with the recipient.

- **Professional Language**: Avoid slang, overly casual language, and emoticons in professional emails or messages. These can undermine the professional quality of your communication.

- **Attention to Detail**: Proofread your messages for spelling, grammar, and punctuation errors. A well-crafted message reflects your competence and attention to detail.

Always approach digital communications as if they were a formal record of your professional behavior. Use professional salutations, maintain a polite and respectful tone, and ensure your message is well-organized and free of errors. This professionalism will contribute positively to your online presence and professional reputation.

Responding Promptly

The immediacy of digital communication has led to heightened expectations for quick responses. Prompt replies are seen as a sign of professionalism and respect in business contexts and are appreciated in personal communications as well. Delays in responding can be misconstrued as a lack of interest or professionalism, potentially harming relationships and business opportunities.

Strategies for Timely Responses

- **Acknowledgment**: If you cannot provide a detailed response immediately, acknowledge the receipt of the message and indicate when the sender can expect a reply. This shows that you value their communication and are attentive to their needs.

- **Scheduling**: Set aside specific times during your day to check and respond to emails and messages. This can help manage the expectation of immediacy while ensuring you do not become overwhelmed by constant communication demands.

Develop a system for managing your digital communications that allows you to respond promptly without sacrificing the quality of your work or personal time. Use automated responses if you will be unavailable for extended periods, informing senders when they can expect a reply. Prioritize messages based on urgency and importance to ensure that critical communications are addressed in a timely manner.

Privacy and Security

In the digital age, the importance of safeguarding privacy and security cannot be overstated. The ease with which information can be disseminated online poses significant risks, especially when it comes to personal or confidential data. Cyber threats like phishing, malware, and data breaches further exacerbate these concerns, making vigilance essential.

Implementing Best Practices

- **Confidentiality Measures**: Utilize encryption and secure communication platforms, especially when exchanging sensitive information. Tools like VPNs (Virtual Private Networks) and encrypted messaging apps can provide additional layers of security.

- **Awareness and Caution**: Stay informed about common cyber threats and the tactics used by cybercriminals. Be cautious about the information you share online and the links or attachments you open.

- **Verification**: Before sharing sensitive information, verify the identity of the recipient. This is particularly important in professional contexts where impersonation or fraudulent requests could lead to significant losses.

Always prioritize the privacy and security of your digital communications. This means choosing secure platforms, being mindful of the information you share, and staying vigilant against potential cyber threats. Regularly updating your knowledge on cybersecurity practices and tools can also help protect your and others' sensitive information.

Digital Etiquette

Digital etiquette, or netiquette, plays a critical role in maintaining respectful and constructive online interactions. Given the diversity of platforms and the global nature of digital communication, understanding the nuances of netiquette becomes crucial. This includes recognizing the appropriate tone, language, and behavior for different online environments, from professional emails to social media platforms.

Guidelines for Good Digital Etiquette

- **Respect and Empathy**: Approach all digital interactions with respect and empathy. Consider how your words might affect others, remembering that behind every screen is a person with their own feelings and perspectives.

- **Appropriate Behavior**: Avoid behaviors that could be perceived as aggressive or disrespectful, such as using all caps (which can be interpreted as shouting), spamming, or posting inappropriate content.

- **Platform Norms**: Each digital platform has its own set of norms and expectations. Familiarize yourself with these conventions to ensure your interactions are appropriate and respectful.

Reflect before you communicate digitally, considering the impact of your words and actions. Practicing good digital etiquette not only fosters positive interactions but also builds a respectful online community. When in doubt, err on the side of caution and professionalism, especially in mixed or unknown audiences.

Managing Misunderstandings

Misunderstandings are a common challenge in digital communication, where the lack of visual and tonal cues can lead to misinterpretation of messages. Such misunderstandings can escalate conflicts or create tension if not addressed promptly and with sensitivity.

Strategies for Resolving Misunderstandings

- **Proactive Communication**: If a misunderstanding arises, address it directly by clarifying your intent and seeking to understand the other party's perspective. This can often defuse potential conflicts and clear up confusion.

- **Medium Switch**: For complex or sensitive issues, switching to a more personal communication medium (such as a phone call or video chat) can facilitate better understanding and resolution.

- **Apology and Empathy**: If your message has been misinterpreted, offer a sincere apology and explain your intended meaning. Showing empathy towards the other person's feelings can help mend misunderstandings and preserve relationships.

Always approach potential misunderstandings with a mindset geared towards resolution and understanding. Suggesting a switch to a more personal communication medium can be particularly effective in resolving issues that arise from digital miscommunications. Maintaining a calm, respectful tone throughout the process is key to successful resolution and maintaining positive digital interactions.

Chapter Three: Emotional Intelligence

Emotional Intelligence (EI) is a multifaceted concept that has garnered substantial attention in psychology and communication fields for its critical role in determining success in personal and professional life. Unlike traditional intelligence quotients (IQ) that focus on cognitive abilities, EI encompasses the ability to recognize, understand, manage, and use emotions effectively in oneself and others.

Components of Emotional Intelligence

Emotional intelligence is broadly categorized into four core skills, which are further divided into two primary competencies: personal competence and social competence.

Self-Awareness:

- Personal Competence

- Self-awareness is the foundational element of EI, involving the ability to recognize and understand one's own emotions, strengths, weaknesses, values, and drives. This awareness is crucial for self-confidence and self-assessment.

Self-Regulation:

- Personal Competence

- Following self-awareness, the ability to manage or regulate one's emotions appropriately is vital. Self-regulation encompasses self-control, trustworthiness, conscientiousness, adaptability, and innovation. It enables individuals to respond to situations rather than react impulsively.

Social Awareness:

- Social Competence

- This component involves understanding the emotions, needs, and concerns of others, picking up on emotional cues, and feeling comfortable socially. It includes empathy, organizational awareness, and service orientation. Social awareness allows for more effective and empathetic communication and relationship-building.

Relationship Management:

- Social Competence

- The ability to manage interactions and relationships, inspire and influence others, manage conflict, and work well in a team are aspects of relationship management. This skill builds on the previous three, utilizing an understanding of one's own emotions and those of others to interact positively and effectively.

Importance of Emotional Intelligence

The significance of emotional intelligence in both personal and professional realms cannot be overstated. Here are some of the key areas where EI has a profound impact:

- **Professional Success**: High EI is correlated with better job performance. Managers and leaders with high emotional intelligence are better at handling stress, leading teams, and fostering a positive work environment, which translates to higher productivity and satisfaction among employees.

- **Relationships**: Emotional intelligence is fundamental in developing and maintaining healthy relationships. It enhances communication, empathy, and understanding, allowing for stronger connections and more effective conflict resolution.

- **Mental and Emotional Well-being**: Individuals with high EI are better equipped to manage stress, navigate challenges, and avoid anxiety and depression. They possess a greater capacity for self-regulation, which contributes to overall mental health.

- **Leadership**: Emotional intelligence is a key attribute of effective leadership. Leaders with high EI can inspire trust, communicate vision, and motivate others more effectively, fostering a sense of loyalty and commitment among their followers.

- **Adaptability**: The rapidly changing modern work environment requires adaptability and resilience—qualities that are closely linked to emotional intelligence. Those with high EI are more adaptable to change, open to innovation, and capable of managing uncertainties.

Self-Awareness: Recognizing and Understanding Your Emotions

Self-awareness, the cornerstone of emotional intelligence, involves recognizing and understanding one's own emotions and their impact on thoughts and behavior. It is the first step toward mastering emotional intelligence, enabling individuals to navigate their internal emotional landscape with clarity and insight.

Self-awareness is the ability to identify and comprehend one's emotions as they occur, along with the ability to recognize their influence on thoughts, behaviors, and interactions with others. It requires a conscious effort to tune into one's emotional state and understand the root causes of these emotions.

Strategies for Enhancing Self-Awareness:

Mindfulness Practice

Mindfulness is a practice that roots an individual firmly in the present, inviting an open and non-judgmental awareness of one's thoughts, feelings, and bodily sensations. It is an intimate journey into the self that illuminates the landscape of our internal experiences, revealing the intricate patterns of our emotional life. Engaging regularly in mindfulness can sharpen one's self-awareness, offering a clearer understanding of personal emotional responses and the subtle shifts within our internal state. To weave mindfulness into the fabric of daily life, one can start with simple yet profound exercises such as mindful breathing, meditation, or yoga. These practices serve not only as gateways to inner tranquility but also as tools for deepening our connection with ourselves, encouraging a harmonious balance between mind and body. By setting aside time each day for these exercises, we invite a greater awareness and appreciation of the present moment, fostering a space where self-discovery and emotional insight can flourish.

Journaling

Journaling stands as a reflective mirror, offering a space to candidly explore our thoughts and emotions. It is a personal dialogue, a means to dissect and understand our emotional experiences and the narratives we construct around them. By consistently dedicating time to journaling, we engage in a process of self-exploration, tracing the contours of our emotional landscapes. This practice allows for an introspective examination of our reactions to various events, illuminating recurring emotional patterns and triggers. Through the act of writing, we process and sift through our feelings, gaining clarity and insights that might otherwise remain obscured. This deliberate reflection can reveal areas ripe for growth and transformation, encouraging a deeper emotional understanding and a more nuanced self-awareness.

The Value of Seeking Feedback

Feedback from others serves as a valuable lens through which we can view ourselves from an external vantage point. It offers a fresh perspective on our behaviors and emotional reactions, shedding light on aspects of ourselves that we may be blind to. Engaging in conversations with trusted friends, family, or colleagues, and inviting their honest feedback, can be a transformative experience. It requires an openness to receive and reflect upon their observations, a willingness to confront uncomfortable truths, and a commitment to personal growth. This process of seeking and integrating feedback into our self-understanding can unveil blind spots in our self-perception, enriching our self-awareness and fostering a deeper, more rounded understanding of ourselves.

Expanding Our Emotional Vocabulary

The words we use to describe our emotions play a crucial role in our ability to understand and communicate our inner experiences. A rich and varied emotional vocabulary enables us to pinpoint and articulate our feelings with precision, offering clarity both to ourselves and to those with whom we communicate. Engaging with a broader lexicon of emotion words can enhance our emotional literacy, allowing for a more accurate and nuanced expression of our internal states. By learning and practicing the use of diverse emotional terms, we deepen our understanding of the multifaceted nature of our feelings, fostering a greater self-awareness and facilitating more effective interpersonal communication.

Recognizing Physical Signals of Emotions

Our emotions are intricately linked with physical sensations in the body, and learning to recognize these signals can provide valuable insights into our emotional well-being. Physical manifestations of emotions, such as tension, changes in heart rate, or stomach butterflies, act as indicators of our internal emotional landscape. By attuning ourselves to these physical cues, we can gain early awareness of our emotional states, opening the door to more effective emotional management. This practice of observing and interpreting the physical sensations associated with emotions encourages a holistic approach to understanding ourselves, integrating body and mind in the pursuit of self-awareness and emotional intelligence.

Managing Emotions: Strategies for Self-Regulation

Following the path laid out by self-awareness, the journey of emotional intelligence progresses to managing emotions, or self-regulation. This critical component involves the ability to control and direct one's emotional responses in a healthy and productive manner. Self-regulation is not about suppression or denial of emotions but rather understanding them and choosing how to act on them. It enables individuals to handle stress, navigate conflicts, and adapt to change with resilience. Moreover, it underpins the ability to set and achieve personal and professional goals by staying focused and motivated.

Pause Before Responding

Reacting impulsively to emotionally charged situations often leads to regrettable decisions or escalates conflicts. Taking a moment to pause before responding allows you to engage your rational mind, giving you the opportunity to choose a more measured and appropriate reaction. This pause can be the difference between a response that fosters understanding and one that exacerbates a problem.

Implementing the Practice of Pausing

- **Mindfulness Techniques**: Incorporate mindfulness techniques such as deep breathing or counting to ten. These practices can help lower immediate emotional reactions and clear your mind for a more rational assessment of the situation.

- **Objective Assessment**: Use the pause to ask yourself key questions about the situation. What are the facts? How might the other person be feeling? What is the most constructive outcome I can aim for? This helps shift your focus from emotional reaction to solution-oriented thinking.

Cultivate a habit of intentionally pausing before reacting, especially in situations that evoke strong emotions. This practice not only aids in emotional regulation but also enhances your ability to communicate effectively and maintain healthy relationships. Over time, this habit will become more automatic, significantly improving your interpersonal interactions and decision-making processes.

Identify Emotional Triggers

Emotional triggers can be specific words, tones, behaviors, or situations that evoke a strong emotional reaction. These triggers are often rooted in past experiences, making them personal and sometimes difficult to anticipate. By identifying and understanding your emotional triggers, you can better prepare for and navigate situations that might otherwise lead to heightened stress or conflict.

Regularly reflect on interactions or events that led to strong emotional responses. What common factors can you identify? Recognizing patterns helps in pinpointing your triggers.

Keeping a journal of your emotional reactions can provide insights into the triggers and your typical responses. Over time, this record can reveal patterns and help you understand your emotional landscape more clearly.

Once you've identified your triggers, develop strategies for managing your response when they're activated. This might include taking a pause, using calming techniques, or preparing rational responses ahead of time. Awareness of your triggers and practicing alternative responses can greatly enhance your emotional intelligence and resilience.

Practice Cognitive Reappraisal

Cognitive reappraisal is a powerful technique in emotional regulation, allowing you to reinterpret a situation in a way that changes your emotional response to it. This doesn't mean ignoring your emotions or the reality of a situation but rather finding a more balanced or positive perspective that reduces emotional distress.

How to Practice Cognitive Reappraisal

- **Reframing the Situation**: Actively look for alternative interpretations or positive angles in a challenging situation. For example, a work setback can be seen as an opportunity for learning and growth rather than just a failure.

- **Empathy and Perspective-Taking**: Consider the situation from the perspective of others involved. This can help reduce personal biases and emotional reactions, fostering a more empathetic and comprehensive understanding of the situation.

Regularly practice reframing your thoughts about situations that typically elicit negative emotions. This practice not only helps in the moment but also strengthens your cognitive flexibility over time, making it easier to manage emotional responses in a variety of situations. Cognitive reappraisal can significantly contribute to your overall well-being and effectiveness in interpersonal relationships.

Develop Coping Strategies

Coping strategies are vital for managing stress, anxiety, and other challenging emotions. They provide a way to navigate through difficult times by helping to restore a sense of balance and control. Effective coping strategies can vary widely among individuals, as what works for one person may not work for another. The key is to find and develop practices that resonate with you and can be reliably accessed when needed.

Implementing Effective Coping Strategies

- **Diverse Activities**: Incorporate a range of activities that promote relaxation and well-being. This can include physical exercise, which reduces stress hormones and stimulates endorphin production; creative pursuits, which can serve as a form of expression and distraction; and mindfulness practices like meditation, which help center your thoughts and emotions.

- **Social Support**: Leverage your social network for emotional support. Conversations with friends or loved ones can offer new perspectives, emotional comfort, and direct assistance in managing your feelings.

- **Routine Integration**: Make these activities part of your regular routine, not just methods to turn to in times of crisis. This regular practice strengthens your emotional resilience, making it easier to handle stress when it arises.

Actively explore various coping mechanisms to identify the ones that effectively help you manage stress and emotional upheaval. Once identified, practice these strategies regularly to make them more effective when you need them. Remember, it's also important to be flexible and adapt your strategies as your needs and circumstances change.

Set Clear Goals and Values

Setting clear goals and underlying values provides direction and purpose, serving as a stabilizing force during emotional upheavals. Goals give you something to strive for, focusing your energies and efforts on productive activities, while values help ensure that your actions align with your deeper beliefs and principles. This alignment can contribute to a sense of fulfillment and reduce the frequency and intensity of emotional distress.

Creating and Using Goals and Values

- **Personal Reflection**: Spend time reflecting on what is most important to you. What do you want to achieve in your life? What principles do you want to live by? These reflections can help you identify your core values and set meaningful goals.

- **Specific, Measurable Goals**: Make your goals specific, measurable, achievable, relevant, and time-bound (SMART). This clarity makes it easier to track progress and stay motivated.

- **Value-Driven Decisions**: Use your values as a guide for making decisions, especially when facing emotional challenges. Ask yourself whether a potential action aligns with your values and contributes to your long-term goals.

Regularly review and adjust your goals and values to ensure they remain relevant and motivating. Use them as a compass to navigate emotional challenges, making decisions that are congruent with who you are and who you aspire to be. This process of continual reflection and adjustment can help maintain emotional balance and drive personal growth.

Empathy: Developing Sensitivity to Others' Emotions

Empathy, is the capacity to understand and share the feelings of others. It goes beyond mere sympathy to a deep, emotional resonance that allows one to truly comprehend what another person is experiencing. Empathy fosters deeper connections, enhances communication, and facilitates conflict resolution.

Empathy involves two key components: cognitive empathy (the ability to understand another person's perspective) and emotional empathy (the ability to physically feel what another person feels). A third aspect, compassionate empathy, combines understanding and feeling to motivate actions that help relieve another person's suffering. Empathy bridges gaps between individuals, promoting a sense of trust and mutual understanding.

Developing Empathy:

Perspective-Taking

Perspective-taking is an essential skill for fostering empathy and understanding in social interactions. It involves the conscious effort to step into another person's shoes, to see the world from their vantage point, and to grasp their unique thoughts and feelings. This mental exercise not only enriches your cognitive empathy but also bridges the gap between differing viewpoints, fostering a sense of connection and understanding. By imagining oneself in another's situation, it becomes possible to comprehend the reasons behind their actions and reactions, taking into account their personal background, life experiences, and the specific context of their behavior.

To practice perspective-taking effectively, it is vital to actively engage in the process during interactions with others. This means making a deliberate effort to consider their perspective by pondering what they might be experiencing emotionally and mentally. Questions such as "What could be influencing their thoughts right now?" or "How might their life experiences shape their reaction to this situation?" can guide this practice. This approach encourages empathy and a deeper connection by acknowledging the complexity of individual experiences and the variety of factors that influence people's perceptions and emotions.

Emotional Mirroring

Emotional mirroring is a technique that can significantly enhance emotional connections with others. It involves observing and reflecting the emotions that another person is displaying through their expressions, body language, and vocal tones. By subtly mirroring these emotional signals, you create a non-verbal dialogue that communicates understanding and empathy. This practice can facilitate a stronger emotional bond and a sense of shared experience, as it signals to the other person that their feelings are seen and validated.

The best practice for emotional mirroring includes being attentive to the subtle cues that others express emotionally. It's about more than just copying facial expressions or gestures; it's about genuinely connecting with the emotion behind those expressions. For instance, if someone is showing signs of sadness, reflecting a compassionate and concerned demeanor can make them feel supported and understood. This practice requires sensitivity and authenticity to be effective, ensuring that the mirroring comes across as genuine empathy rather than mimicry.

Cultivating Curiosity about Others

Curiosity about others is a cornerstone of building empathy. By fostering a genuine interest in what makes people tick—their thoughts, feelings, and life stories—you pave the way for deeper connections and understanding. This curiosity encourages an open-minded approach to interactions, where the goal is to learn and understand rather than to judge or advise.

Practicing this involves engaging others in conversations that go beyond superficial topics. Asking open-ended questions that prompt them to share more about their experiences, feelings, and thoughts is key. This not only conveys that you value their perspective but also that you are willing to listen and understand. Listening intently without interrupting or rushing to provide solutions allows for a richer exchange of ideas and emotions, fostering a climate of mutual respect and understanding.

Seek Diverse Experiences

Exposing yourself to a broad range of cultures, perspectives, and life stories is crucial for developing a well-rounded sense of empathy. Diverse experiences enrich your understanding of the human condition, highlighting the vast array of challenges, joys, and viewpoints that people encounter. By stepping out of your comfort zone and engaging with stories and individuals that differ from your own background, you challenge your preconceptions and expand your capacity for empathy.

This can be achieved by consuming media from various cultures, participating in community events that celebrate diversity, or simply having conversations with people from different backgrounds. Each of these experiences serves as a window into another way of life, offering insights into the feelings and thoughts of others. The key is to approach these experiences with an open heart and mind, ready to learn and grow from the encounters. This openness not only broadens your perspective but also deepens your ability to empathize with others, regardless of their background or experiences.

Chapter Four: Problem-Solving and Decision-Making

Critical Thinking

Critical thinking is the disciplined process of actively analyzing, synthesizing, and evaluating information gathered from observation, experience, reflection, reasoning, or communication. It is foundational to effective problem-solving, enabling individuals to make reasoned judgments that are logical and well-thought-out. Critical thinking involves questioning assumptions, evaluating evidence, and considering alternative perspectives. It goes beyond mere problem-solving to encompass the ability to analyze complex issues, identify logical connections, and derive conclusions not immediately apparent. Critical thinkers are skeptical of information presented to them, seeking to understand the underlying principles and motivations before drawing conclusions.

So, step by step:

1. Identify and Clearly Define the Problem:

The initial phase of any effective problem-solving process involves the accurate identification and precise definition of the problem at hand. This crucial step is more than just recognizing that a problem exists; it's about understanding the nature of the issue in depth. A problem well defined is considered to be halfway solved because once you have a clear grasp of what you're dealing with, the path to finding a solution becomes much clearer. To achieve this clarity, the "5 Whys" technique is invaluable. This method entails asking "Why?" repeatedly, usually five times, to peel away the superficial layers of a problem and reach its core. Each "Why?" is designed to explore the cause-and-effect relationships underlying the problem. By the time you've asked "Why?" for the fifth time, you should have uncovered the fundamental root cause of the issue. This depth of understanding is critical for guiding the subsequent steps in the critical thinking and problem-solving process effectively.

2. Gather Relevant Information:

The next step in critical thinking and problem-solving is the collection of relevant information. This stage is about conducting thorough research to gather all necessary data that could potentially help solve the problem. It involves a variety of activities such as reading up on the topic, observing the problem or related processes in action, and consulting with experts or stakeholders. The goal is to accumulate a comprehensive set of information from credible and reliable sources. Embracing diversity in your sources is a best practice in this phase; it ensures that you obtain a wide range of perspectives on the issue, which can help in identifying aspects of the problem you may not have considered. It's also important to critically evaluate each source for reliability and bias, as working with accurate and unbiased information is crucial for making informed decisions. This careful selection and assessment of information lay the groundwork for effective analysis and solution development.

3. Analyze the Information:

With a wealth of relevant information at your disposal, the next step is to analyze this data to discern patterns, relationships, and potential solutions. This analytical phase is where you break down the collected information into more manageable parts, making complex data easier to understand and interpret. Tools and methodologies like SWOT analysis can be instrumental during this phase. A SWOT analysis helps in evaluating the Strengths, Weaknesses, Opportunities, and Threats related to the problem, offering a structured way to assess both the internal and external factors that could impact the solution. Additionally, mind mapping can be an effective technique for organizing and visually representing the information, relationships, and hierarchies within the data. By creating a visual representation of the problem and its related factors, you can more easily see how different pieces of information are connected and how they might influence potential solutions. This systematic and thorough analysis is key to identifying viable solutions and making informed decisions as you move forward in the problem-solving process.

4. Think Logically and Creatively:

Logical thinking grounds your approach in reason and evidence, enabling you to deduce solutions that are rational and based on available data. On the other hand, creative thinking encourages you to explore beyond conventional boundaries, to discover novel and innovative solutions that might not be immediately apparent. This duality of thought processes ensures a comprehensive approach to problem-solving, combining the reliability of logic with the boundless potential of creativity.

The practice of encouraging both divergent and convergent thinking is a best practice in this context. Divergent thinking involves brainstorming a wide array of solutions without pre-emptive judgment or criticism, allowing for a free flow of ideas and encouraging creativity. Once a broad set of potential solutions has been identified, convergent thinking is then applied. This is a process of narrowing down the options, using logical analysis to evaluate the feasibility and effectiveness of each idea, ultimately selecting the most promising solutions for further exploration or implementation. This balanced approach ensures that problem-solving efforts are both imaginative and grounded, leading to innovative yet practical solutions.

5. Evaluate Alternatives and Implications:

Once a set of potential solutions has been generated through logical and creative thinking, the next step involves a thorough evaluation of these alternatives, considering their potential outcomes and implications. This critical analysis is about more than just identifying a viable solution; it's about understanding the broader impact of each option, including the pros and cons, as well as the short-term and long-term effects of implementation. This comprehensive evaluation ensures that the chosen solution is not only effective in addressing the immediate problem but also sustainable in the long run.

A decision matrix serves as an invaluable tool in this phase. This systematic approach allows you to objectively evaluate each potential solution against a set of predefined criteria that are relevant to the situation at hand. By assigning weights to these criteria based on their importance and scoring each solution accordingly, you can compare the options on an objective basis. This methodical evaluation helps in making a more informed and rational decision, ensuring that the selected solution optimally addresses the problem within the given constraints.

6. Make a Decision and Act:

With the alternatives evaluated and the implications considered, the next critical step is to make a decision and take decisive action. Decisiveness plays a pivotal role in problem-solving, as it moves the process from the theoretical realm of possibilities into the practical world of action. Even when faced with uncertainty, the ability to make a decision and commit to a course of action is crucial.

Best practice in this phase involves committing to the chosen solution and developing a detailed action plan for its implementation. This plan should outline the steps necessary to put the solution into practice, including timelines, resources needed, and responsible parties. It's also important to remain flexible and adaptive, ready to adjust the plan as new information emerges or as the situation changes. This adaptability ensures that the solution can be refined or redirected as needed to achieve the desired outcome effectively.

7. Reflect and Learn from the Outcome:

The problem-solving process doesn't end with the implementation of a solution; reflection on the process and its outcomes is essential for continuous learning and improvement. This reflective phase involves examining the effectiveness of the solution and the efficiency of the problem-solving process itself. By analyzing what worked well, what didn't, and why, valuable insights can be gained for future endeavors.

Best practice for this final step includes conducting a thorough review after the solution has been implemented, focusing on the process, the outcome, and any unforeseen consequences. Questions to consider include: Were the objectives achieved? What unexpected challenges arose? How could the process be improved? Documenting these reflections and insights ensures that the lessons learned are captured and can inform future problem-solving efforts. This cycle of action and reflection fosters a culture of continuous improvement, enhancing the effectiveness of critical thinking and problem-solving skills over time.

Creative Thinking: Fostering Innovation and Creativity

Creative thinking is the ability to look at problems or situations from a fresh perspective that suggests unorthodox solutions. It involves thinking outside the traditional framework to identify new patterns, alternative ideas, or unique approaches. In an increasingly complex and fast-paced world, the ability to generate innovative solutions is more valuable than ever. Creative thinking fuels progress, drives innovation, and enables individuals and organizations to overcome challenges and capitalize on new opportunities. It is essential not only in artistic endeavors but in every field, from business and science to education and social change.

Strategies for Enhancing Creativity

Cultivate a Creative Mindset: Fostering a creative mindset is essential for unlocking the full potential of your imagination and innovative capabilities. This mindset is characterized by an inherent curiosity about the world, an openness to new experiences, and a playful approach to problem-solving. It invites an exploratory behavior, encouraging individuals to question the status quo, venture beyond the familiar, and consider possibilities that deviate from conventional wisdom. Embracing failure as part of the learning process is crucial; it's viewed not as a setback but as a vital step towards discovery and innovation.

To cultivate such a mindset, it's important to actively challenge existing assumptions and engage in open-ended questioning. Asking "What if?" or "Why not?" can open doors to new ways of thinking and solutions that might not have been considered otherwise. Making curiosity a daily practice—by seeking out new knowledge, exploring unfamiliar subjects, and allowing yourself the freedom to wonder—can significantly enhance your creative thinking. This approach not only broadens your perspective but also deepens your understanding and appreciation of the complexities and interconnectedness of the world around you.

Create a Stimulating Environment: The environment in which you work and create plays a significant role in influencing your creative output. Spaces that are visually stimulating, comfortable, and tailored to minimize distractions can significantly boost your ability to generate innovative ideas. A well-designed environment can inspire creativity, providing the visual cues and comfort needed to foster a productive and imaginative mindset.

Personalizing your workspace with objects or artwork that inspire you can create a constant source of motivation and stimulation. Having easy access to tools and resources that support your creative endeavors—be it through technology, traditional art supplies, or simply space to think and experiment—is also critical. Furthermore, introducing periodic changes to your environment, such as rearranging your workspace or working in new locations, can offer fresh perspectives and spark new ideas. This adaptability encourages the mind to remain active and open to novel concepts and solutions.

Diversify Experiences: Diversity of experience is a powerful catalyst for creativity. Engaging with different cultures, disciplines, and perspectives exposes you to a wide array of ideas, practices, and worldviews, enriching your creative reservoir. This exposure broadens your understanding and appreciation of the world, providing a vast pool of inspiration from which to draw when faced with creative challenges.

Actively seeking out new experiences is key to maintaining a dynamic and expansive creative mindset. This can be achieved through travel, immersing yourself in different cultures, and exploring new environments. Reading extensively across genres and subjects, attending workshops and seminars, and engaging in conversations with individuals from diverse backgrounds and disciplines are all effective ways to broaden your horizons. Each new experience not only adds to your knowledge and skills but also enhances your ability to think creatively by connecting disparate ideas and perspectives in innovative ways.

Encourage Ideation Without Judgment: The foundation of generating creative and novel ideas lies in the ability to freely explore thoughts without the fear of judgment or immediate criticism. This principle is crucial during the early phases of the creative process, where the goal is to generate a wide array of ideas, no matter how unconventional or preliminary they may seem. Creating an environment that supports this free exchange of ideas is essential for unlocking the full creative potential of individuals and teams. Such an environment encourages participants to share their thoughts openly, fostering a culture of innovation and exploration.

Best practices in this area include organizing brainstorming sessions that emphasize the importance of contribution without immediate evaluation. During these sessions, all ideas are documented, acknowledging their potential as seeds for innovation that can be refined and developed further. Employing visual thinking tools like mind mapping can also enhance this process, as it allows for the visual organization of ideas and the exploration of connections between concepts that might initially appear unrelated. This method not only aids in generating a broader range of ideas but also in identifying unique and innovative solutions that might not have emerged through traditional linear thinking processes.

Foster Collaborative Creativity: Collaborative creativity is a powerful approach to innovation, combining diverse viewpoints, skills, and experiences to produce outcomes that might be unattainable by individuals working in isolation. The synergy created through collaboration can significantly amplify the creative output, as team members build on each other's ideas, leading to the cross-pollination of thoughts and the generation of novel solutions. This collaborative approach leverages the collective intelligence of the group, creating a dynamic environment where creativity thrives.

To foster collaborative creativity effectively, it is vital to engage in projects that bring together individuals from a variety of backgrounds and disciplines. Encouraging an open dialogue and the free exchange of ideas within the team is essential, as it ensures that all perspectives are heard and considered. By leveraging the unique strengths and insights of each team member, the group can explore a wider range of solutions and approaches, leading to more innovative and comprehensive outcomes.

Embrace Challenges and Constraints: Contrary to the common perception that constraints hinder creativity, they can actually serve as catalysts for innovation. Limitations force individuals and teams to think more critically and creatively, pushing them to explore solutions within a defined framework. This necessity to operate within boundaries encourages a more focused and inventive approach to problem-solving, as it requires the identification of alternative strategies and solutions that comply with the constraints at hand.

Viewing challenges and constraints as opportunities rather than obstacles is a best practice in creative problem-solving. By embracing these limitations as integral components of the creative process, individuals and teams can use them as springboards for innovation. This approach involves using the constraints as a starting point for brainstorming, encouraging the exploration of unconventional solutions and approaches that might not have been considered in an unconstrained environment. Through this lens, limitations become a valuable tool for stimulating creative thinking and driving the development of unique and effective solutions.

Overcoming Cognitive Biases

Cognitive biases are systematic patterns of deviation from norm or rationality in judgment, whereby inferences about other people and situations may be drawn in an illogical fashion. These biases are influenced by a variety of factors, including personal experience, social norms, and emotional states, and they can significantly impact the decision-making process. Cognitive biases can lead to poor decision-making, misjudgment of situations, and incorrect assessments of risk and probability. Some common biases include:

Confirmation Bias

Confirmation bias represents a fundamental challenge in critical thinking and decision-making. It is the mental tendency to process and prioritize information that aligns with our existing beliefs, opinions, or hypotheses, while simultaneously disregarding or undervaluing evidence that contradicts them. This bias affects how information is gathered, interpreted, and remembered, leading to a skewed perception of reality based on one's preconceived notions. The danger of confirmation bias lies in its ability to create echo chambers, where one becomes insulated from opposing viewpoints, potentially leading to erroneous conclusions and decision-making based on incomplete or selective information.

To mitigate the effects of confirmation bias, it is crucial to actively seek out and consider information and perspectives that challenge your existing beliefs. This involves critical evaluation of sources, engaging with diverse viewpoints, and being open to changing your stance in light of new, credible evidence. Cultivating an awareness of this bias and deliberately questioning your assumptions can lead to more balanced and informed decision-making.

Anchoring Bias

Anchoring bias occurs when an individual relies too heavily on an initial piece of information—the "anchor"—to make subsequent judgments and decisions. This initial information sets a reference point that disproportionately influences the outcome, regardless of the relevance or accuracy of new information that emerges. Anchoring can significantly impact both trivial and major decisions, from estimating the value of an item to making strategic business decisions, often leading to skewed outcomes that do not accurately reflect the full scope of available data.

Combatting anchoring bias requires awareness and deliberate effort to question initial impressions and estimates. It involves seeking additional information and perspectives to challenge the initial anchor and adjusting decisions based on a more comprehensive understanding of the situation. Encouraging a culture of reflection and critical evaluation before settling on decisions can help to reduce the influence of anchoring bias.

Overconfidence Bias

Overconfidence bias describes the tendency of individuals to overestimate their own abilities, knowledge, and capacity to predict outcomes accurately. This bias can lead to a false sense of security and certainty in one's decisions and predictions, often ignoring the real risks and uncertainties involved. Overconfidence can result in underpreparation, overlooking potential challenges, and making decisions based on overly optimistic assumptions, which can have significant negative consequences in various contexts, from personal life to professional decision-making.

To counter overconfidence bias, it is beneficial to adopt a more humble and questioning approach to knowledge and decision-making. This includes acknowledging the limits of one's knowledge, seeking feedback and advice from others, and considering a range of outcomes, including those that may not align with one's initial expectations. Incorporating systematic and structured decision-making processes, such as scenario planning and risk assessment, can also help in providing a more realistic understanding of uncertainties and the range of possible outcomes.

Availability Heuristic

The availability heuristic is a mental shortcut that relies on immediate examples that come to a person's mind when evaluating a specific topic, concept, method, or decision. This heuristic often leads to a distorted assessment of prevalence or probability, as individuals tend to overestimate the likelihood of events that are more recent, memorable, or emotionally impactful. This can skew risk assessment and decision-making processes, leading to decisions based on vivid memories rather than statistical realities.

Reducing the impact of the availability heuristic involves making a conscious effort to base decisions on objective data and statistical evidence rather than anecdotal or highly memorable examples. It also helps to broaden one's sources of information to include a wider range of experiences and data points. Seeking out and considering the actual statistical likelihood of events can provide a more accurate basis for decision-making, rather than relying solely on the most readily available memories or stories.

Strategies for Overcoming

Awareness and Education: The foundational step in mitigating the influence of cognitive biases on our decision-making process is the cultivation of awareness and education about these biases. Recognizing that cognitive biases exist and understanding how they can subtly influence our perceptions and judgments is crucial. This awareness acts as the first line of defense against the automatic and often unconscious application of these biases. By educating ourselves and those around us about the nature and effects of various cognitive biases, we empower individuals to identify moments when their thinking may be skewed by such predispositions.

Best practices in this area involve a proactive approach to learning about common cognitive biases and reflecting on how these biases may have played a role in past decisions. This reflection can illuminate patterns of thought that may have led to suboptimal outcomes, providing valuable lessons for future decision-making. Incorporating discussions and training sessions on cognitive biases in team environments can also help cultivate a collective awareness, allowing team members to hold each other accountable and support each other in overcoming these biases.

Seek Diverse Perspectives: One of the most effective ways to counteract the influence of personal biases is by integrating diverse perspectives into the decision-making process. Diverse viewpoints bring a range of experiences, knowledge, and ways of thinking that can challenge and expand our own understanding. By actively seeking input from people who come from different backgrounds, have varied experiences, and possess distinct areas of expertise, we introduce a broader spectrum of considerations into our discussions.

Best practices for leveraging diverse perspectives include making a conscious effort to include individuals from a variety of disciplines, cultures, and professional backgrounds in decision-making processes. This can be facilitated through structured brainstorming sessions, collaborative projects, or consultation processes designed to gather insights from a wide array of stakeholders. Encouraging an environment where diverse opinions are not only welcomed but also valued is key to unlocking the full potential of this approach, as it ensures that all voices are heard and considered in the pursuit of more balanced and informed decisions.

Challenge Assumptions: Challenging underlying assumptions is critical in reducing the impact of cognitive biases on our judgments and decisions. Assumptions can act as invisible barriers that shape our thinking and conclusions, often without our conscious awareness. By critically examining and questioning these assumptions, we can uncover hidden biases and ensure that our decisions are grounded in reality and evidence, rather than unchecked beliefs or flawed premises.

Best practices for challenging assumptions include fostering a culture of inquiry where questioning is encouraged as part of the decision-making process. Regularly engaging in exercises that ask, "What assumptions are we making? Are they justified?" can help bring these underlying beliefs to the surface. This practice encourages a more deliberate and reflective approach to decision-making, prompting individuals and teams to critically evaluate the basis of their reasoning. Ensuring that this questioning becomes an integral part of the decision-making framework can significantly enhance the quality and robustness of the outcomes, making them more resilient to the distortive effects of cognitive biases.

Foster an Environment of Psychological Safety: Creating a workplace culture that values psychological safety is essential for combating cognitive biases and fostering effective team dynamics. Psychological safety refers to an environment where individuals feel confident and encouraged to share their thoughts, opinions, and concerns without fear of embarrassment, ridicule, or retribution. This kind of environment is crucial for enabling team members to express dissenting views or question decisions, which can play a pivotal role in identifying and addressing cognitive biases that may affect decision-making processes.

Best practices for fostering psychological safety include actively promoting open dialogue and constructive criticism. Leaders and team members alike should work to establish norms that encourage the expression of concerns and alternative viewpoints in a respectful and supportive manner. By ensuring that all team members have the opportunity to voice their perspectives, teams can leverage the full range of their collective insights and experiences, helping to uncover blind spots or biased thinking that may otherwise go unchallenged.

Slow Down the Decision-Making Process: The pace at which decisions are made can significantly influence the likelihood of cognitive biases impacting the outcome. When decisions are rushed, there is a greater chance that biases such as availability heuristics, anchoring, or confirmation bias will skew judgment and lead to suboptimal choices. Slowing down the decision-making process allows individuals and teams the time needed to thoroughly consider all aspects of a decision, evaluate a wider range of alternatives, and deliberate on the potential consequences of each option.

Best practices for moderating the pace of decision-making include allocating sufficient time for complex or significant decisions and introducing a "cooling-off" period. This period allows decision-makers to step back from their initial judgments and reassess their choices after some time has passed, providing an opportunity to view the decision from a different perspective and potentially identify biases or oversights.

Chapter Five: Teamwork and Collaboration

Roles and Relationships

The dynamics of teamwork encapsulate the complex interplay of roles, relationships, and interactions that occur within a team. Effective teamwork is not just about bringing people together; it's about aligning individual strengths and weaknesses, establishing clear roles, fostering positive relationships, and creating an environment where everyone can contribute toward a common goal. In any team, members assume various roles that contribute to the group's overall function and success. These roles can be formally assigned or naturally adopted based on individual skills, preferences, and personalities. Dr. Meredith Belbin's Team Roles theory identifies nine roles that individuals tend to take on within teams, including:

The Plant: Creative and innovative, the Plant is crucial for generating fresh ideas and approaches. This role is characterized by a high level of creativity and imagination, often serving as the source of inspiration for new projects or solutions. Plants thrive on solving complex problems with original thinking, though they may require support to refine and implement their ideas effectively. Their innovative perspective is vital in keeping the team dynamic and forward-thinking.

The Resource Investigator: With an extroverted nature, the Resource Investigator excels in exploring opportunities and networking with others. This role involves reaching out beyond the team to bring in ideas, information, and developments that can provide valuable insights or advantages. Resource Investigators are adept at negotiating with stakeholders and leveraging external contacts, making them key players in ensuring the team has access to the resources and support it needs.

The Coordinator: Serving as a chairperson, the Coordinator is pivotal in clarifying goals and delegating tasks, ensuring that the team's efforts are aligned with its objectives. Coordinators excel in understanding team members' strengths and are skilled at assigning responsibilities that maximize individual contributions. Their leadership is essential in steering the team towards its goals, providing direction and motivation.

The Shaper: The Shaper is the driving force that challenges the team to improve and overcome obstacles. Characterized by their determination and courage, Shapers possess the energy and passion to push the team forward, especially when faced with challenges or tight deadlines. Their ability to inject urgency and drive can be crucial in maintaining momentum and achieving results, though they may need to balance their intensity to maintain team harmony.

The Monitor Evaluator: This role is focused on providing strategic and critical insights, with a talent for judging situations accurately. Monitor Evaluators are analytical and discerning, able to assess options objectively and identify the most viable solutions. Their contributions are invaluable in strategic planning and decision-making, ensuring that the team's actions are grounded in solid reasoning and evidence.

The Teamworker: Supportive and cooperative, the Teamworker plays a key role in fostering team unity and ensuring collaborative efforts. Teamworkers are empathetic and diplomatic, often acting as the glue that holds the team together, smoothing over conflicts and ensuring that all members feel valued and understood. Their focus on harmony and cooperation is essential for maintaining a positive team atmosphere and facilitating effective collaboration.

The Implementer: Practical and reliable, the Implementer is the one who turns ideas into actions and organizes work. With a focus on efficiency and pragmatism, Implementers are adept at planning and executing tasks, ensuring that projects are carried out effectively. Their organizational skills and attention to operational details are critical in translating the team's plans into tangible results.

The Completer Finisher: With an eye for detail, the Completer Finisher ensures that tasks are carried out thoroughly and to a high standard. This role is characterized by a dedication to quality and an aversion to errors, making Completer Finishers crucial in maintaining the quality of the team's output. Their meticulous nature helps to catch and correct mistakes before they become problematic, ensuring that deliverables are polished and complete.

The Specialist: Specialists bring a depth of knowledge and expertise in a particular area, providing the team with specialized skills and insights. Their expert understanding can be critical in navigating complex challenges that require specific technical knowledge or skills. While Specialists focus on their area of expertise, their contributions can be pivotal in achieving objectives that require specialized understanding or capabilities.

Fostering Positive Relationships

The relationships between team members significantly impact the team's ability to collaborate effectively. Positive relationships are characterized by trust, respect, and open communication. They enable team members to feel valued and supported, encouraging a sense of belonging and commitment to the team's objectives.

Strategies for Building Positive Team Relationships:

1. Communicate Openly and Effectively: Encouraging open and effective communication within a team sets the stage for a transparent and inclusive culture. This means creating an environment where team members feel comfortable voicing their ideas, concerns, and feedback without fear of judgment or reprisal. Achieving this requires regular, structured meetings where all members have the opportunity to speak and contribute. Additionally, maintaining open lines of communication outside of these meetings—through various channels like email, messaging apps, and informal catch-ups—ensures that dialogue continues to flow freely. This open communication framework supports problem-solving, decision-making, and innovation, as it allows for the free exchange of ideas and information.

2. Build Trust: Trust is the cornerstone of any successful team. It is cultivated through consistent, reliable behavior and decision-making, underpinned by a foundation of integrity. Team members who trust each other are more likely to collaborate effectively, share openly, and support one another's efforts. Building trust involves keeping commitments, being transparent about processes and decisions, and showing respect for colleagues' contributions and concerns. As trust deepens, the team's resilience and ability to tackle complex challenges together grow stronger.

3. Respect Diversity: Diversity within teams brings a wealth of perspectives and skills, which can significantly enhance creativity, problem-solving, and innovation. Respecting and valuing the diverse backgrounds and viewpoints of team members involves actively listening to and considering their ideas and experiences. This respect for diversity should be woven into the team's culture, from the way meetings are conducted to how decisions are made. Recognizing the unique contributions of each team member and leveraging these differences in a constructive way can lead to more creative and effective solutions.

4. Encourage Collaboration: A collaborative team environment is one where members actively work together towards common goals, recognizing that each person's contribution is vital to the team's success. Promoting collaboration involves not just encouraging team members to share ideas and resources but also creating systems and processes that facilitate joint effort. This could include collaborative tools for project management, shared digital workspaces, and regular team-building activities that foster a sense of unity and shared purpose. When collaboration is a core part of the team's operation, it can lead to more efficient problem-solving and a more positive work atmosphere.

5. Resolve Conflicts Constructively: Conflict is a natural part of teamwork, arising from differences in opinions, approaches, or personalities. However, when approached constructively, conflicts can lead to growth, innovation, and stronger relationships. Constructive conflict resolution focuses on addressing the issue at hand rather than resorting to personal attacks. This involves clear communication, empathy, and a willingness to understand different perspectives. Establishing norms for conflict resolution within the team, such as active listening, seeking common ground, and focusing on solutions, can help manage disagreements in a way that strengthens the team rather than dividing it.

Effective Collaboration

Effective collaboration goes beyond mere cooperation to involve deep synergy, where the collective effort produces a greater outcome than the sum of individual contributions:

Creating a Shared Vision and Objectives

The cornerstone of effective teamwork and collaboration is a unified vision and clear, mutually agreed-upon objectives. This common purpose ensures that all team members are moving in the same direction, with a shared understanding of what they are working towards. It transforms individual efforts into a collective drive towards achieving specific goals.

Best Practice: Initiating this shared understanding can begin effectively with a kickoff meeting dedicated to establishing and articulating the team's vision and objectives. This meeting is not just a formality but a crucial step in building commitment and alignment among team members. It's an opportunity to discuss, refine, and agree upon the goals that will guide the team's efforts. To maintain focus and motivation, it's equally important to regularly revisit these goals, ensuring they remain relevant and are clearly communicated as the project progresses.

Establishing Clear Roles and Responsibilities

Defining clear roles and responsibilities within a team eliminates confusion, prevents task overlap, and ensures efficient use of resources. It allows team members to concentrate on their specific areas of expertise and understand how their contributions fit into the larger picture.

Best Practice: Adopting a structured framework like RACI (Responsible, Accountable, Consulted, Informed) can significantly clarify individual roles and responsibilities. This clarity helps each team member grasp their specific duties and the expectations placed upon them, thereby enhancing accountability and efficiency. Ensuring everyone has a comprehensive understanding of their role and its importance to the team's success is fundamental to fostering a sense of ownership and engagement.

Fostering Open Communication

The lifeline of collaborative effort is open, honest, and effective communication. It's not just about transmitting information but also about listening, understanding, and integrating diverse viewpoints.

Best Practice: To promote this level of communication, regular team meetings and individual check-ins should be institutionalized. Employing modern collaboration tools that facilitate seamless communication is crucial, especially in accommodating remote or distributed team dynamics. Establishing communication norms—such as expected responsiveness—ensures that all team members feel valued and heard, creating a conducive environment for sharing ideas and feedback.

Leveraging Diversity

A team's strength often lies in its diversity, bringing together varied perspectives, skills, and problem-solving approaches. This diversity is a powerful asset in driving innovation and creativity.

Best Practice: Actively encourage each team member to bring their unique perspectives and experiences into the team's operations. Cultivating an inclusive atmosphere where different viewpoints are not only welcomed but are integral to decision-making processes, enriches the team's collective output and fosters a culture of respect and mutual learning.

Utilizing Collaborative Tools and Technologies

In an increasingly digital landscape, leveraging the right tools and technologies is essential for enhancing teamwork, particularly when managing remote or distributed teams.

Best Practice: Selecting collaborative tools should be a thoughtful process, focusing on the specific needs of the team and project. From project management software to communication platforms and document sharing tools, the chosen technology should facilitate, not complicate, team interaction. Providing necessary training and support ensures all team members can effectively utilize these tools, thereby maximizing the team's collaborative potential.

Encouraging Continuous Feedback

Feedback is a catalyst for growth and improvement in any team setting. A culture of open, constructive feedback allows teams to refine their processes, address challenges, and enhance collaboration over time.

Best Practice: Establish a routine of regular feedback sessions that enable team members to share insights on what's working and areas for improvement. Approaching feedback with a focus on specific actions and behaviors, rather than personal criticism, fosters a positive environment for continuous development and learning.

Adapting and Being Flexible

Flexibility and adaptability are key to navigating the complexities of collaborative projects. Teams that can adjust their plans and strategies in response to new information or challenges are more likely to overcome obstacles and find innovative solutions.

Best Practice: Cultivating a team culture that values flexibility and the willingness to embrace change is vital. Encouraging team members to view challenges as opportunities rather than setbacks promotes a proactive approach to problem-solving and ensures the team remains resilient and dynamic in the face of change.

Conflict Resolution: Strategies for Managing Disputes

Conflict is an inevitable aspect of teamwork and collaboration. Differences in opinions, personalities, and working styles can lead to disputes that, if not managed properly, can undermine the team's effectiveness and morale. However, when approached constructively, conflict resolution can lead to growth, innovation, and strengthened relationships. Before diving into resolution strategies, it's crucial to understand that not all conflicts are detrimental. Distinguishing between constructive conflict, which can stimulate creativity and innovation, and destructive conflict, which can erode team cohesion, is essential. Encourage an environment where constructive disagreement is welcomed but ensure it's based on tasks or ideas, not personal attacks. Recognizing the difference helps in applying the appropriate conflict resolution strategy.

Well, now let's move on to strategies:

Open Communication and Active Listening

Central to resolving conflicts and fostering a harmonious work environment is the practice of open communication coupled with active listening. Open communication allows all parties involved in a conflict to express their views in a transparent manner, ensuring that each perspective is heard. Active listening enhances this process by requiring listeners to fully concentrate, understand, respond, and then remember what is being said. This form of listening is not passive but an active engagement with the speaker, aiming to grasp the essence of their message without premature judgment or interruption.

Best Practice: To implement this effectively, organize structured discussions where each participant has a designated time to speak without interruptions from others. This structured approach ensures that all voices are heard and valued equally. Following up with a summary or paraphrase of the points made by each speaker can significantly aid in confirming that messages have been correctly understood. This practice not only clarifies any misunderstandings but also validates the speakers by showing that their points have been acknowledged and considered.

Identify the Underlying Causes

Conflicts are seldom about the surface issue but rather stem from deeper, underlying causes such as unmet needs, perceived injustices, or fundamental miscommunications. Addressing only the symptoms of a conflict without understanding its root causes is unlikely to lead to a sustainable resolution. Therefore, identifying these underlying issues is crucial for effectively resolving conflicts in a way that addresses the core concerns of all parties involved.

Best Practice: Engage in a process of inquiry and reflection to uncover the real issues driving the conflict. This involves asking probing questions that encourage individuals to reflect on and express the deeper reasons behind their positions or grievances. Looking beyond the immediate disagreement to understand the fundamental needs or concerns can reveal the true nature of the conflict, facilitating a more effective and lasting resolution.

Focus on Interests, Not Positions

A common obstacle in conflict resolution is the tendency for parties to become entrenched in their positions, making it difficult to find a mutually acceptable solution. However, when the focus shifts from positions (what someone wants) to interests (why they want it), it becomes easier to identify common ground and explore solutions that satisfy the underlying needs of all parties.

Best Practice: Encourage each party involved in the conflict to express their interests related to the disagreement. This can be facilitated through open-ended questions that prompt individuals to consider and articulate the needs, desires, or concerns driving their positions. By understanding the interests at play, parties can move beyond binary opposition and work collaboratively towards creative solutions that address the core motivations of each side. This interest-based approach fosters a more cooperative and empathetic atmosphere, paving the way for innovative and mutually beneficial resolutions.

Develop Integrative Solutions

Integrative solutions represent a pinnacle in conflict resolution strategies, where the focus shifts from competing interests to finding solutions that benefit all parties involved. Unlike compromises, which often involve each side making concessions, integrative solutions aim for outcomes where everyone feels they have gained something of value. This approach requires a deep understanding of the underlying interests of all parties and a commitment to exploring a wide range of potential solutions.

Best Practice: To foster integrative solutions, initiate brainstorming sessions dedicated to generating multiple options for resolving the conflict. Encourage creative and open-ended thinking, allowing for the exploration of solutions that might initially seem unconventional. Each proposed solution should then be evaluated not just for its feasibility but for how well it aligns with the interests and needs of all parties involved. This process of collective problem-solving not only increases the chances of finding a mutually beneficial resolution but also strengthens the collaborative spirit among the parties.

Embrace a Collaborative Attitude

A collaborative attitude transforms conflict resolution from a confrontational process into an opportunity for growth, relationship building, and process improvement. By viewing conflicts as shared challenges to overcome, rather than battles to be won, parties can reduce defensiveness and foster a more productive dialogue. This shift in mindset is critical for moving away from a zero-sum perspective, where one party's gain is seen as another's loss, towards a more cooperative approach.

Best Practice: Cultivate a team-oriented environment where the common goal is to resolve the conflict to everyone's benefit. This involves actively promoting the notion that all team members are on the same side, working together to find the best possible outcome. Encouraging this sense of unity and shared purpose can significantly reduce resistance and promote a more open, constructive exchange of ideas.

Seek External Mediation if Necessary

When internal efforts to resolve a conflict reach an impasse, or when the situation is particularly complex or charged, involving an external mediator can provide a fresh, impartial perspective. External mediators, whether HR professionals, trained conflict resolution specialists, or other neutral third parties, bring a level of detachment and objectivity that can be difficult to achieve from within the conflict.

Best Practice: If deciding to seek external mediation, it's essential to choose a mediator who is perceived as neutral and respected by all parties involved. The mediator's role is to facilitate communication, help clarify the underlying issues, and guide the parties towards a mutually acceptable resolution. Ensuring that the mediator's approach and methodology are trusted and accepted by all involved is crucial for the success of the mediation process.

Establish Agreements and Follow-Up

A clear, written agreement that outlines the resolution and the specific actions each party will take is a cornerstone of effective conflict resolution. Such agreements formalize the commitment to the resolution, set expectations for all involved, and provide a framework for assessing the implementation of the solution.

Best Practice: Draft a detailed agreement that captures the essence of the resolution and the steps to be taken by each party. This document should be reviewed and agreed upon by all parties to ensure clarity and commitment. Additionally, scheduling regular follow-up meetings is crucial for monitoring the progress of the agreement's implementation, allowing for adjustments as needed, and addressing any new or residual issues that may arise. This ongoing dialogue ensures that the resolution is actively maintained and that the relationships continue to be built on a foundation of trust and mutual respect.

Building and Maintaining Trust in Teams

Trust is the bedrock upon which effective teams are built. It fosters open communication, enhances collaboration, and creates a safe environment where innovation and creativity can flourish. Trust within a team not only improves productivity but also contributes to a positive and supportive work culture.

Trust in a team context refers to the confidence among team members that their peers' intentions are good and that there is no reason to be protective or cautious around the group. When trust is present, team members feel comfortable being vulnerable, taking risks, and expressing their thoughts and opinions without fear of judgment or retribution.

Lead by Example

Leaders are instrumental in setting the tone for the team's culture, including how trust is built and maintained. By embodying trustworthiness in their actions—through consistency, transparency, and integrity—leaders demonstrate the value of trust in interpersonal and professional relationships. This example serves as a powerful model for team members, emphasizing that trust is a foundational element of the team's operations.

Align your actions with your words to reinforce trustworthiness. Be open about how decisions are made, readily admit mistakes, and consistently fulfill your commitments. This transparency and reliability not only set a standard for the team but also encourage a culture where trust is reciprocated and valued.

Show Respect and Appreciation

Acknowledging and valuing each team member's contributions is a vital component of building trust. Recognition of hard work and achievements, both on an individual level and as a team, reinforces the message that every member's effort is crucial to the team's success.

Regularly acknowledge team achievements and individual contributions. Provide feedback in a manner that is both respectful and constructive, ensuring that team members feel valued and understood. Celebrating successes and recognizing the effort behind every task can significantly boost morale and trust within the team.

Encourage Vulnerability

A culture where vulnerability is embraced is one where trust flourishes. When leaders and team members feel safe to share their challenges, failures, and uncertainties, it creates a deeper sense of connection and mutual trust.

Lead by example by sharing your own experiences of vulnerability and encouraging others to do the same. Cultivate an environment where mistakes are seen as opportunities for growth rather than reasons for criticism. This approach not only deepens trust but also promotes a learning culture within the team.

Promote Reliability

Trust is closely tied to reliability. When team members consistently meet their commitments and support one another, it reinforces the reliability of the team as a whole. This reliability is a cornerstone of trust, ensuring that team members feel confident in their collective ability to achieve goals.

Clearly communicate responsibilities and expectations regarding deadlines and commitments. Foster an atmosphere of mutual accountability where team members feel supported in their efforts to meet their obligations. Holding each other accountable in a constructive manner strengthens trust and reinforces the team's commitment to its goals.

Facilitate Strong Relationships Among Team

Trust is rooted in personal connections and understanding. By encouraging team members to build relationships beyond work-related tasks, leaders can foster a sense of camaraderie and mutual respect that is essential for trust.

Organize team-building activities that allow team members to interact in a more relaxed and informal setting. Encourage social interactions outside of work tasks, providing opportunities for team members to discover common interests and form deeper bonds. These personal connections serve as the foundation for a trusting and cohesive team.

Chapter Six: Adaptability and Flexibility

In an era defined by rapid technological advancements, globalization, and constant change, adaptability has emerged as a critical skill for individuals and organizations alike. Adaptability—the ability to adjust to new conditions—enables us to navigate the complexities and uncertainties of the modern world.

Adaptability involves a willingness to confront the unknown, to let go of the familiar, and to embrace change. It is characterized by flexibility in thinking, openness to new ideas, and the capacity to modify one's approach in response to evolving circumstances. An adaptable individual sees change not as a threat but as an opportunity for growth and learning.

The Significance of Adaptability

Professional Success and Career Growth: The professional landscape is dynamic, with technological advancements and market demands leading to the constant evolution of job roles and industries. Adaptability empowers individuals to navigate these changes successfully, allowing them to seize new opportunities, transition across career paths, and continuously update their skill set. This agility is not just about surviving the changes but thriving in them, fostering innovation, and contributing creatively to one's field.

Commit to lifelong learning by actively seeking out professional development opportunities. This can include attending workshops, enrolling in courses related to emerging technologies or methodologies, and staying informed about industry trends. Being proactive about career development and open to shifting career paths as opportunities arise ensures sustained relevance and success in the workforce.

Personal Development: Adaptability on a personal level is about embracing change as an integral part of growth and self-improvement. It encourages an open-minded approach to experiences and challenges, fostering resilience and the capacity to cope with and learn from life's ups and downs. This flexibility in thinking and being allows for a more enriching and fulfilling life experience.

Develop a growth mindset by viewing challenges as opportunities to learn and expand your capabilities. Approach new situations and obstacles with curiosity and resilience, seeing them as paths to personal growth rather than barriers to success.

Social and Cultural Integration: In our interconnected and globalized world, adaptability is key to navigating diverse social and cultural landscapes. It enables individuals to understand and appreciate different perspectives, fostering empathy and the ability to form meaningful connections across cultural divides. This skill is invaluable in both personal and professional contexts, where cultural competence can enhance communication and collaboration.

Actively engage with diverse communities and cultures through travel, language learning, and participation in cultural events. Approach these experiences with openness and respect, aiming to understand different ways of life and perspectives.

Resilience in the Face of Change: Life is inherently unpredictable, and adaptability is crucial for maintaining resilience in the face of constant change. Whether dealing with personal setbacks, professional shifts, or broader societal changes, the ability to adapt ensures that individuals can navigate uncertainty with confidence and emerge stronger from challenges.

Focus on developing flexible coping strategies that embrace change. Concentrate on aspects of your life that you can control, and maintain a positive outlook towards the future. Building a support network and practicing self-care are also vital components of a resilient approach to life's inevitable changes.

Strategies for Enhancing Adaptability

Develop Emotional Intelligence: Emotional intelligence is a critical component of adaptability, enabling individuals to effectively understand and manage their own emotions as well as perceive and influence the emotions of others. This skill set is particularly valuable in times of change, as it aids in navigating the emotional complexities and challenges that often accompany new situations. By recognizing and regulating one's own emotional responses, individuals can maintain clarity and focus, making more informed decisions amidst uncertainty. Furthermore, understanding the emotions of others can facilitate better communication and collaboration, essential qualities for adapting to new environments or circumstances. Enhancing emotional intelligence involves self-reflection, seeking feedback, and practicing empathy, all of which contribute to a more adaptable and resilient mindset.

Seek Varied Experiences: Exposure to a diverse range of experiences is a powerful way to build adaptability. By stepping outside of one's comfort zone and engaging with new ideas, cultures, and challenges, individuals can significantly broaden their perspectives. This diversity of experience not only encourages flexibility in thought and behavior but also fosters a more inclusive worldview. Varied experiences challenge preconceived notions and habitual ways of thinking, pushing individuals to develop new problem-solving strategies and creative approaches to obstacles. Actively seeking out new experiences, whether through travel, learning new skills, or simply engaging in unfamiliar activities, cultivates a mindset that is more open to change and better equipped to handle the unexpected.

Practice Mindfulness: Through mindfulness, individuals can cultivate a heightened awareness of their thoughts, feelings, and surroundings, allowing them to respond to changes with greater calm and clarity. This present-moment awareness prevents being overwhelmed by future uncertainties or past regrets, enabling a more adaptable and proactive approach to life's challenges. Practicing mindfulness can involve meditation, mindful breathing exercises, or simply integrating mindful awareness into daily activities. Over time, this practice can significantly improve one's ability to remain flexible and responsive in the face of change.

Cultivate a Support Network: Having a robust support network is invaluable in enhancing adaptability. Friends, family, mentors, and colleagues can provide essential emotional support, practical advice, and different perspectives during times of change. This support network acts as a sounding board, offering encouragement and feedback that can help individuals navigate transitions more smoothly. Moreover, a diverse support network can introduce new ideas and opportunities, further encouraging adaptability. Building and maintaining strong relationships requires effort and openness, including the willingness to offer support to others in return. Actively engaging in community groups, professional associations, or social activities can expand one's network, providing a richer source of support and inspiration for adaptability.

Flexibility: Strategies for Managing Change

Flexibility, a key component of adaptability, is the capacity to adjust one's thoughts, behaviors, and actions in response to changing circumstances. It letting go of previous plans or ideas when necessary and embracing the possibility of new outcomes. This quality is crucial for innovation, problem-solving, and resilience.

Strategies for Enhancing Flexibility

Cultivate a Growth Mindset: A growth mindset, a concept developed by psychologist Carol Dweck, is foundational to adaptability. It is the understanding that abilities and intelligence can be developed through dedication, hard work, and a love of learning. This mindset contrasts with a fixed mindset, where abilities are seen as innate and unchangeable. A growth mindset encourages individuals to embrace challenges, persevere in the face of setbacks, and view effort as a path to mastery. It transforms obstacles into opportunities for growth, fostering resilience and a proactive approach to learning.

To cultivate a growth mindset, start by reevaluating how you perceive challenges and failures. Instead of seeing them as insurmountable barriers or proof of incapacity, view them as opportunities to learn and improve. Embrace challenges with enthusiasm and persistence, understanding that every setback is a chance to develop resilience and enhance your capabilities. Celebrate progress and effort over perfection, and encourage this perspective in others as well.

Develop Emotional Agility: Emotional agility is a skill that involves being flexible with your thoughts and feelings in a way that empowers you to respond optimally to everyday situations. It is the ability to experience your emotions without being controlled by them, allowing you to make choices that align with your values and intentions. Emotional agility enables individuals to navigate life's twists and turns with self-awareness, compassion, and an open mind.

Cultivating emotional agility starts with recognizing and labeling your emotions as you experience them. When faced with strong emotions, take a moment to pause and reflect rather than reacting impulsively. Ask yourself what these emotions are telling you about your needs, values, or perceptions. By approaching your feelings with curiosity and without judgment, you can gain insights into your emotional triggers and patterns. Use these insights to guide your actions in a way that is constructive and aligned with your goals.

Expand Your Comfort Zone: Stepping out of your comfort zone is a practical approach to building adaptability. It involves deliberately putting yourself in new or challenging situations that provoke a certain degree of discomfort. By regularly pushing your boundaries, you increase your tolerance for uncertainty and become more adept at handling change. This process strengthens your ability to adapt by forcing you to develop new coping strategies and perspectives.

Begin expanding your comfort zone by setting small, achievable goals that challenge your current boundaries. This could be anything from taking a public speaking course to traveling solo for the first time. The key is to start with manageable challenges and gradually increase the difficulty as your confidence grows. Celebrate these accomplishments, no matter how small, as each step outside your comfort zone contributes to greater flexibility and adaptability. By continuously seeking growth and embracing the unfamiliar, you can cultivate a more adaptable and resilient approach to life's challenges.

Plan for Multiple Outcomes: The ability to adapt to change is significantly enhanced by preparing for a variety of potential outcomes. While it's important to have a clear plan in place, the recognition that the future is inherently uncertain—and that plans may need to change—is equally crucial. By anticipating different scenarios and considering what actions would be necessary under each, you can build a flexible strategy that allows for quick pivots and adjustments without losing momentum.

Start by identifying key goals or projects and then brainstorm possible outcomes, ranging from the most likely to the least expected. For each scenario, develop a set of contingency plans or actions that could be taken to address the challenges or opportunities presented. This might involve setting aside resources, such as time or finances, that can be allocated as needed, or developing skills that will be valuable in various circumstances. By planning for multiple outcomes, you're not just preparing to react to changes; you're positioning yourself to proactively manage them, reducing stress and enhancing your ability to navigate the unknown.

Seek Diverse Perspectives: Flexibility is also cultivated by exposing oneself to a wide range of ideas and viewpoints. Engaging with diverse perspectives challenges existing assumptions and encourages a more open-minded approach to problem-solving and decision-making. By understanding and valuing different ways of thinking, you can unlock new possibilities and solutions that would not have been apparent from a more homogeneous viewpoint.

Actively seek out voices and opinions that differ from your own. This can be achieved through a variety of channels, such as joining cross-disciplinary professional groups, attending cultural events, or simply having conversations with individuals from different backgrounds. Reading widely and consuming media that offers alternative viewpoints can also broaden your understanding and appreciation of diversity. Embracing diverse perspectives not only enhances your adaptability but also enriches your personal and professional life with deeper insights and more creative solutions.

Learning Agility: Embracing New Skills and Knowledge

Learning agility is the ability to quickly absorb new information, learn new skills, and apply them effectively in various situations. Learning agility enables individuals to stay relevant, competitive, and innovative. It is not just about acquiring knowledge for its own sake but about applying it creatively in new contexts. Agile learners are better equipped to handle complexity, solve problems, and adapt to new challenges.

Strategies for Enhancing Learning Agility

Cultivate a Curiosity Mindset: Curiosity is a powerful force for personal and professional growth, driving individuals to seek out new knowledge, experiences, and perspectives. It is the foundation of a lifelong learning habit that can open doors to new opportunities and ideas. Cultivating a curiosity mindset means actively pursuing questions and interests, even—and especially—when they fall outside your usual scope of knowledge or expertise. This mindset encourages an exploratory approach to life and work, where learning and discovery are valued for their own sake.

To foster a curiosity mindset, consciously dedicate time to exploring new subjects, hobbies, or skills that intrigue you. Approach these explorations with a "beginner's mind," setting aside any preconceptions or assumptions you might have. This openness can lead to a deeper and more nuanced understanding of the world around you, sparking further interest and curiosity. Engaging with diverse sources of information and seeking out experiences that challenge your current perspectives can also enrich your curiosity and adaptability.

Embrace Challenges as Learning Opportunities: Challenges and setbacks are inevitable in both personal growth and professional development. However, by reframing these experiences as opportunities for learning, you can cultivate resilience and a positive outlook on the process of overcoming obstacles. This shift in perspective transforms challenges from discouraging roadblocks into valuable lessons that contribute to your growth and adaptability. Viewing challenges in this light encourages a proactive and persistent approach to problem-solving and personal development.

Whenever you encounter a challenge, pause to consider the learning opportunities it presents. Ask yourself questions like, "What can this situation teach me?" or "How can I grow from this experience?" By focusing on the potential for growth and development, you can maintain motivation and find innovative solutions to overcome obstacles. Documenting these experiences and the lessons learned can further solidify your growth mindset and enhance your ability to adapt to future challenges.

Practice Reflective Learning: Reflective learning is a deliberate process of thinking critically about your experiences, analyzing your actions, and considering how you can improve or apply the lessons learned in future situations. This practice deepens your understanding of both successes and failures, enabling you to make more informed decisions and adapt more effectively to new challenges.

Maintain a learning journal where you regularly reflect on your experiences, the outcomes, and the lessons you've drawn from them. This could include reflections on professional projects, personal challenges, or any new learning endeavors. Consider what worked well, what didn't, and how you can apply this knowledge moving forward. Regularly reviewing and reflecting on these entries can provide valuable insights into your learning patterns and areas for growth, further enhancing your adaptability and resilience.

Engage in Continuous Skill Development: As industries evolve and new technologies emerge, the demand for specific skills can shift dramatically. Staying ahead in your career requires a commitment to continuous learning and skill development. This proactive approach to personal and professional growth ensures that you not only keep pace with changes in your field but also position yourself as a valuable asset capable of adapting to new challenges and opportunities.

Start by conducting a self-assessment to identify any skill gaps or areas for improvement that align with current trends in your industry. Set specific, achievable goals for skill development, and seek out resources that can help you meet these objectives. This might include enrolling in relevant online courses, attending workshops and seminars, or dedicating time to self-study and practice. Regularly updating your skills keeps you competitive in the job market and prepared for future advancements in your field.

Leverage Cross-Disciplinary Learning: Innovation often occurs at the intersection of disciplines, where diverse perspectives and approaches can lead to creative solutions. Cross-disciplinary learning broadens your knowledge base and enhances your problem-solving skills by exposing you to different ways of thinking and doing. This approach not only fosters innovation but also equips you with a more versatile skill set, making you more adaptable to changes and challenges that may arise.

Actively seek out learning opportunities beyond your primary area of expertise. This could involve taking courses in related fields, participating in interdisciplinary projects, or simply engaging with literature and media from a variety of disciplines. Look for ways to integrate these new insights into your current work or study, exploring how concepts from one area can inform and improve practices in another. The ability to draw connections between disparate fields can lead to unique innovations and a competitive edge in your career.

Adopt a Flexible Learning Style: Adaptability in learning is not just about what you learn but also how you learn. Embracing a flexible approach to learning enables you to effectively acquire and apply knowledge in various formats and settings. This flexibility ensures that you can continue to learn and grow, even as the modes and methods of education evolve.

Challenge yourself to step outside your comfort zone by trying new learning methodologies. If you typically rely on reading and note-taking, consider incorporating more interactive or hands-on learning experiences, such as workshops, simulations, or practical projects. Take advantage of the wealth of learning resources available online, including webinars, podcasts, and educational videos. By diversifying your learning approaches, you not only discover what methods best suit your learning style but also enhance your ability to adapt to and embrace new ways of acquiring knowledge.

Coping with Stress: Techniques for Resilience

Stress is the body's response to any demand or challenge, which can be triggered by both positive and negative experiences. Resilience, on the other hand, is the ability to bounce back from stress, adversity, failure, or challenges. While a certain level of stress can be motivating, excessive stress can impair our ability to function effectively and enjoy life. It's not about avoiding stress but learning how to deal with it effectively.

Techniques for Coping with Stress and Building Resilience

Physical Activity: Engaging in regular physical activity is one of the most effective ways to combat stress. Exercise not only has a positive impact on your physical health but also promotes mental well-being by reducing levels of the body's stress hormones, such as adrenaline and cortisol. It also stimulates the production of endorphins, the brain's natural mood elevators and painkillers. Moreover, exercise can improve sleep, which is often disrupted by stress, creating a cycle of stress and sleep issues.

To reap the stress-relief benefits of exercise, choose activities that you genuinely enjoy and can look forward to. This could be anything from brisk walking or jogging to swimming, cycling, yoga, or team sports. The key is consistency; incorporating physical activity into your daily routine, even in small amounts, can make a significant difference in managing stress levels. Setting achievable fitness goals can also provide a sense of accomplishment and further reduce stress.

Social Support: Having a robust network of supportive relationships is invaluable in managing stress. Social support provides an outlet for sharing feelings and concerns, offering both emotional comfort and practical assistance. Strong social connections are linked to a host of positive health outcomes, including lower levels of anxiety and depression, higher self-esteem, and greater empathy.

Cultivate and maintain close relationships with family, friends, and colleagues. Make an effort to connect regularly, whether in person, over the phone, or through digital means. Be open to sharing your experiences and feelings, and equally, be a supportive presence for others in their times of need. Participating in community groups, clubs, or online forums can also expand your social network and provide additional sources of support and companionship.

Time Management: Effective time management is a critical skill for reducing stress and enhancing productivity. By prioritizing tasks, setting realistic goals, and organizing your schedule, you can avoid the overwhelm that often accompanies a packed or disorganized agenda. Good time management not only helps in accomplishing tasks more efficiently but also frees up time for relaxation and self-care activities that can further reduce stress.

Start by prioritizing tasks based on urgency and importance, and plan your day or week accordingly. Set realistic deadlines and break larger tasks into smaller, manageable steps. Incorporate regular short breaks into your schedule to rest and recharge, as continuous work without breaks can increase stress. Learning to delegate tasks when possible and saying no to additional commitments that could lead to overloading your schedule are also essential aspects of effective time management.

Positive Thinking and Optimism: Embracing a positive mindset is a powerful tool in the stress management arsenal. Optimism, in this context, is not about denying the existence of problems or challenges.

Instead, it's about maintaining a belief in your ability to overcome obstacles and viewing setbacks as temporary and surmountable. This approach helps in framing challenges not as insurmountable barriers but as opportunities to apply your skills and grow. A positive outlook encourages resilience, making it easier to navigate through tough times with a sense of hope and confidence in your ability to manage.

Practicing gratitude is a practical way to cultivate a positive mindset. Keeping a gratitude journal, where you regularly record things you're thankful for, can significantly shift your focus from what's going wrong to what's going right. This practice can illuminate the often overlooked positives in your life, enhancing your overall sense of well-being. By acknowledging the good, however small, and viewing challenges through a lens of learning and growth, you reinforce optimism and build a stronger, more resilient outlook on life.

Learning to Accept What You Cannot Change: A key aspect of effective stress management is recognizing the difference between what is within your control and what isn't. Stress often arises from a sense of helplessness in the face of uncontrollable circumstances. Learning to accept that some situations are beyond your control can alleviate unnecessary stress and redirect your energy towards areas where you can make a difference. Acceptance doesn't mean resignation or passivity; it's about acknowledging reality in a way that frees you to focus on influencing the aspects of your life that you can change.

Practicing acceptance involves a conscious effort to let go of the desire for control over uncontrollable events. This can be challenging, as it requires a shift in perspective and, often, a change in habitual responses to stress. Techniques such as mindfulness meditation, cognitive-behavioral strategies, or even professional counseling can be helpful in fostering this acceptance. By concentrating on what you can influence and releasing the need to control everything, you can reduce feelings of helplessness and anxiety, making it easier to cope with stress in a healthy and productive manner.

Chapter Seven: Leadership and Influence

Leadership is a multifaceted discipline that blends personal attributes, situational awareness, and the ability to influence others toward achieving common goals. An effective leader understands that there is no one-size-fits-all approach to leadership; rather, it's about identifying and developing a style that resonates with their personality, values, and the needs of their team and organization.

Leadership styles can be broadly categorized into several types, each with its own set of characteristics, strengths, and potential drawbacks. Some of the most commonly recognized styles include:

Autocratic Leadership: Autocratic leadership is characterized by strong, centralized control over all decision-making processes, with little to no input from team members. Leaders who adopt this style typically make decisions based on their judgment and perspectives, often under the premise that quick, decisive action is needed. While this can be beneficial in scenarios where rapid decision-making is critical—such as during a crisis or in high-stakes environments—it may not always yield the best long-term results. Over time, the autocratic approach can lead to decreased team morale and motivation, as team members may feel undervalued and overlooked. Their creativity and potential contributions are stifled since there is little room for their ideas or feedback. Although effective in certain contexts, leaders who rely heavily on autocracy should be mindful of these potential drawbacks and consider incorporating more inclusive decision-making practices when possible.

Democratic Leadership: In contrast to autocratic leadership, democratic leadership is grounded in the principles of participation and consensus. Democratic leaders actively seek the input, opinions, and feedback of their team members, valuing diverse perspectives and collaborative problem-solving. This leadership style promotes a sense of equity and belonging among team members, enhancing their engagement and commitment to the team's goals. However, while democratic leadership is beneficial for fostering a positive team environment and encouraging creativity, it may sometimes slow down the decision-making process. Reaching consensus can be time-consuming, particularly in diverse teams with varying opinions. Despite this, the democratic approach often leads to more thoroughly considered decisions and higher levels of team satisfaction, making it a highly effective leadership style in environments where innovation and team cohesion are paramount.

Transformational Leadership: Transformational leadership goes beyond mere transactional exchanges and seeks to inspire and motivate team members towards achieving a higher level of performance and personal growth. Transformational leaders are characterized by their ability to articulate a compelling vision of the future, inspire trust and confidence, and encourage innovation and creativity. They focus on developing the strengths and abilities of their team members, pushing them to exceed their own expectations and contribute to the organization's success in meaningful ways. This leadership style is particularly effective in dynamic and competitive environments where adaptability and continuous improvement are key. By fostering a culture of empowerment and personal development, transformational leaders can achieve remarkable outcomes, driving both team satisfaction and exceptional performance.

Transactional Leadership: Transactional leadership is grounded in the principle of exchanges between the leader and their followers. It is a traditional leadership style that focuses on clear structures, defined roles, and the use of rewards and punishments to motivate performance. Transactional leaders set specific goals and provide direct feedback based on the achievement of these objectives. While this approach can be effective in achieving short-term goals and maintaining a clear sense of order and discipline, it may not foster long-term loyalty or drive innovation within the team. The emphasis on extrinsic motivation might limit the development of intrinsic motivation among team members, potentially stifling creativity and reducing the team's ability to adapt to new challenges. To mitigate these limitations, transactional leaders may benefit from incorporating elements of other leadership styles that encourage more personal growth and team cohesion.

Servant Leadership: Servant leadership flips the traditional leadership model on its head, placing the leader in a role of service to their team. Servant leaders prioritize the well-being and development of their team members, striving to meet their needs and empower them to achieve their full potential. This leadership style is characterized by empathy, listening, and a strong commitment to supporting others. By focusing on the growth and well-being of team members, servant leaders can build strong, cohesive teams that are highly motivated and loyal. However, this approach may require leaders to sometimes put their own interests and immediate goals aside for the benefit of the team and its members. While servant leadership can lead to high levels of team satisfaction and long-term success, leaders must balance the needs of their team with organizational objectives to ensure effective performance.

Situational Leadership: Situational leadership is a dynamic and flexible approach that recognizes the need for leaders to adjust their style based on the context and the maturity level of their team members. Situational leaders assess the needs of their team and adapt their level of direction and support accordingly. This might involve taking a more directive approach with less experienced team members or adopting a delegative style as individuals become more competent and confident. The ability to accurately evaluate situations and adapt leadership behavior is crucial for the success of this style. Situational leadership can be highly effective across a variety of contexts, as it allows leaders to meet their team members where they are and provide the specific guidance and support needed to achieve success. However, it requires a deep understanding of individual team members and the flexibility to change leadership approaches as situations evolve.

Identifying Your Leadership Approach

So, the way to effective leadership starts with a deep understanding of your inherent leadership style. This involves introspection and reflection on your natural tendencies, values, and preferred methods of interacting with others. To gain a clearer picture, consider the feedback from peers, mentors, and team members about your leadership approach and its effectiveness. Reflecting on the outcomes of your previous leadership experiences can also provide valuable insights. This initial step is crucial as it lays the foundation for your growth and development as a leader. By identifying your natural leadership style, you can begin to understand how best to leverage your strengths and address areas for improvement.

Developing Your Leadership Style

Self-awareness: Self-awareness is a key component of effective leadership. It involves a continuous process of reflection on your strengths, weaknesses, and the impact your leadership style has on others. Cultivating self-awareness requires actively seeking feedback from those around you and being open to personal growth and development. By understanding your own capabilities and limitations, you can make more informed decisions, improve your leadership approach, and foster a more positive and productive work environment. Regular self-reflection and feedback are instrumental in this process, as they help you to remain aligned with your values and goals while being responsive to the needs of your team.

Adaptability: Effective leadership demands adaptability. Recognizing that no single leadership style suits all situations is crucial. The ability to adapt your approach based on the specific task at hand, the dynamics of your team, and evolving circumstances can significantly enhance your effectiveness as a leader. This might involve shifting from a more directive approach to a collaborative one, or vice versa, depending on what the situation requires. Developing adaptability as a leader means being open to change, willing to learn, and flexible in your strategies and methods. It's about finding the balance between maintaining your core leadership values and being responsive to the needs of your team and the demands of the environment.

Communication Skills: At the heart of effective leadership lies the ability to communicate effectively. This encompasses not only articulating your vision and expectations clearly but also listening actively to your team members and providing constructive feedback. Good communication skills facilitate better understanding, alignment, and collaboration within the team. They also help in resolving conflicts, building trust, and encouraging a culture of openness and transparency. To improve your communication skills, practice active listening, ensure your messages are clear and concise, and be mindful of non-verbal cues. Effective communication is a two-way street, requiring both speaking and listening with intent and empathy.

Emotional Intelligence: Emotional intelligence is critical for successful leadership. It involves understanding and managing your own emotions as well as recognizing and influencing the emotions of others. High emotional intelligence can lead to better decision-making, improved conflict resolution, and stronger relationships within the team. Key components include empathy, which allows you to understand and share the feelings of others, and social awareness, which helps you navigate the social complexities of the workplace. To cultivate emotional intelligence, work on being more self-aware, practice empathy by putting yourself in others' shoes, and develop your social skills to better connect with and influence your team members.

Motivating Others: Techniques for Inspiring Teams

The ability to motivate others is a crucial skill for leaders seeking to achieve high levels of team performance and satisfaction. Motivation is the force that drives individuals to take action and persist in the face of challenges.

Motivation can be intrinsic, driven by an internal desire to achieve for personal satisfaction, or extrinsic, influenced by external rewards and recognition. Effective leaders recognize the value of both types of motivation and strive to create an environment that nurtures intrinsic motivation while appropriately leveraging extrinsic rewards.

Provide Autonomy and Empowerment: Granting team members autonomy and empowering them to take charge of their tasks and decisions is a transformative approach to leadership. This empowerment not only motivates individuals by giving them a sense of control over their work but also cultivates a culture of trust and responsibility. By aligning delegated tasks and projects with each team member's strengths and interests, leaders can maximize engagement and productivity. Providing the necessary resources and support is crucial to their success, but equally important is stepping back to allow them the space to execute their responsibilities effectively. This balance between offering support and trusting team members to fulfill their roles encourages innovation, as individuals feel free to explore new ideas and approaches within their domain of responsibility.

Offer Constructive Feedback and Recognition: The provision of timely, constructive feedback is vital for personal and professional development. Feedback that clearly communicates areas of strength as well as opportunities for improvement helps individuals understand how their performance aligns with team and organizational goals. Coupled with this, recognition of achievements plays a pivotal role in boosting morale and motivation. Celebrating successes, both in private and public forums, not only acknowledges individual contributions but also reinforces the behaviors and efforts that lead to those achievements. By offering specific, actionable feedback in a manner that is respectful and supportive, leaders can foster a culture of continuous improvement and appreciation, where team members feel valued and inspired to excel.

Foster a Positive Team Culture: The foundation of a highly motivated and engaged team lies in the cultivation of a positive, inclusive culture. Such a culture values collaboration, respect, diversity, and open communication. Creating an environment where every team member feels valued, included, and empowered to share their thoughts and ideas is essential for fostering a sense of belonging and commitment. Encouraging practices that promote mutual respect and support not only enhances team cohesion but also drives collective success. Leaders play a crucial role in modeling these behaviors and setting the tone for the team's interactions, ensuring that the workplace is a space where diversity is celebrated, challenges are approached collaboratively, and successes are shared. Through these efforts, a positive team culture becomes a powerful catalyst for motivation, engagement, and high performance.

Encourage Professional Development: Professional development is not just an avenue for individual team members to enhance their skills and knowledge; it's a clear signal from leadership that the organization is genuinely invested in their future. By providing opportunities for growth and learning, leaders can significantly boost team motivation and engagement. Support can take various forms, such as access to training programs, workshops, seminars, and mentorship opportunities. Encouraging team members to set personal and professional goals, and supporting them in achieving these objectives, demonstrates a commitment to their career progression. This approach not only aids in their personal growth but also benefits the organization by developing a more skilled and versatile workforce. Leaders should foster an environment where continuous learning is valued and where team members feel encouraged to pursue their interests and career aspirations, ultimately contributing to a culture of excellence and innovation.

Understand Individual Motivators: Recognizing that team members are motivated by a variety of factors is crucial for tailoring effective motivational strategies. Individual motivators can vary greatly, ranging from the desire for career advancement and recognition to the need for creative expression or making a meaningful impact. Engaging with team members on a personal level through one-on-one meetings provides valuable insights into their unique goals, challenges, and what drives them. This understanding allows leaders to personalize their approach, aligning motivational strategies with individual aspirations and needs. By taking the time to understand and address the diverse motivators within a team, leaders can foster a highly motivated and engaged workforce, where each member feels valued, understood, and inspired to contribute to their fullest potential.

Influencing Skills: Persuasion and Negotiation Techniques

The ability to influence others is indispensable. It is a critical skill that extends beyond the confines of authority, enabling leaders to navigate complex interpersonal dynamics, foster collaboration, and achieve desired outcomes. Influencing involves persuading or convincing others to understand and embrace your viewpoint or to agree on a mutual course of action.

Persuasion is the process of guiding people toward the adoption of an idea, attitude, or action by rational and emotional means. It is built on the foundation of trust and credibility. Effective persuasion combines the art of communication with the understanding of human psychology.

Key Techniques for Persuasion

Establish Credibility: Credibility is essential in the art of persuasion. It forms the foundation upon which your arguments and proposals are evaluated by others. When you are perceived as trustworthy and knowledgeable, your words carry greater weight, and your ability to influence increases significantly. Establishing credibility involves demonstrating your expertise through your actions, decisions, and how you communicate. It also requires integrity, including the humility to admit when you do not have all the answers and the commitment to seek out and provide those answers when needed. This approach not only builds trust but also reinforces your reputation as a reliable and authoritative source in your field. Consistently displaying these qualities can make you a more effective persuader, as people are naturally inclined to listen to and be influenced by those they respect and trust.

Connect on an Emotional Level: While logical arguments are important, emotional connections often play a critical role in persuasion. People are not solely motivated by facts and figures; their emotions significantly influence their decisions and actions. By understanding and tapping into these emotions, you can make your arguments more compelling and personal. Storytelling is a powerful technique in this regard, as it can vividly illustrate your points and evoke a strong emotional response. Similarly, demonstrating empathy and taking the time to understand the concerns, aspirations, and desires of those you wish to persuade can enhance the effectiveness of your communication. When people feel understood and emotionally connected, they are more likely to be receptive to your message.

Highlight Benefits and Value: Ultimately, individuals are motivated by what they stand to gain or lose in any given situation. Clearly articulating the benefits and value of your proposal is crucial for persuasion. This means tailoring your message to directly address the interests, needs, and concerns of your audience. By effectively communicating the "what's in it for me?" from their perspective, you make your proposal more relevant and appealing. Highlighting the specific advantages and positive outcomes that your audience can expect helps to frame your proposal in a more attractive light. This strategy not only enhances the persuasiveness of your message but also demonstrates your understanding and consideration of your audience's priorities, further reinforcing your credibility and emotional connection with them.

Use Social Proof: Social proof is a powerful psychological phenomenon where people look to the actions and behaviors of others to determine their own. In the context of persuasion, leveraging social proof means providing evidence that others, especially those similar to your audience or respected by them, have endorsed or benefited from your proposal. Sharing success stories, testimonials, or case studies can serve as compelling evidence that your idea or action is valuable and effective. This can help to alleviate doubts or reservations by demonstrating that the proposed action is not only acceptable but also successful in similar contexts. Social proof taps into the natural human tendency to be influenced by the experiences and actions of peers, making it a potent tool in your persuasive arsenal.

Reciprocity: The principle of reciprocity reflects the human tendency to feel obliged to return favors or kindnesses. In persuasion, this means that offering something of value upfront can make others more inclined to listen to and accept your proposals. This could involve providing useful information, assistance, or even making concessions that benefit the other party. By doing so, you create a sense of goodwill and obligation, making it more likely that your audience will be open to your ideas and suggestions. The key is to ensure that what you offer is genuinely valuable and relevant to the other party, reinforcing your credibility and enhancing the receptiveness of your audience to your subsequent proposals. This strategic approach to persuasion fosters a positive dynamic where both parties feel valued and respected, paving the way for more effective and mutually beneficial interactions.

Process of Negotiation

At its core, negotiation is a process of dialogue aimed at reaching an agreement or resolving a dispute between parties with differing needs, desires, or viewpoints. Effective negotiation is not about winning at the expense of the other party but about finding a solution that is acceptable to all involved. This requires a blend of preparation, clear communication, and a genuine effort to understand and accommodate the needs of the other party.

The ability to identify and focus on common ground is paramount, as it provides a basis for building agreements that honor the interests of all parties.

Prepare Thoroughly: The cornerstone of any successful negotiation is thorough preparation. This involves a clear understanding of your own objectives, as well as an appreciation of the needs and goals of the other party. Equally important is the development of a Best Alternative To a Negotiated Agreement (BATNA), which serves as your fallback option should the negotiation not reach an acceptable outcome. Preparation also entails knowing your non-negotiables—those aspects you cannot compromise on—and recognizing areas where flexibility is possible. Conducting comprehensive research on the context and specifics of the negotiation enables you to approach the dialogue with confidence and clarity, armed with the information needed to make informed decisions and proposals.

Listen Actively: Active listening is a vital component of effective negotiation. It goes beyond merely hearing the words of the other party to truly understanding their perspective, concerns, and underlying needs. By listening more than you speak and employing techniques such as reflective listening—where you paraphrase or summarize what you've heard to confirm understanding—you demonstrate respect and a genuine interest in reaching a mutually satisfactory resolution. Active listening fosters an atmosphere of trust and cooperation, making it easier to identify areas of agreement and explore solutions that accommodate the interests of both sides.

Seek Win-Win Outcomes: The goal of any negotiation should be to find solutions that are advantageous for all involved parties. Striving for win-win outcomes not only resolves the immediate conflict or negotiation but also lays the groundwork for positive, ongoing relationships and future collaborations. This approach requires moving beyond rigid positions to explore the underlying interests and needs of both sides. By focusing on these interests, negotiators can identify creative solutions that may not have been apparent at the outset. This might involve brainstorming together to find alternatives that satisfy the most critical needs of each party, thereby ensuring that the agreement is sustainable and valued by all.

Manage Emotions: Negotiations can often become emotionally charged, making it essential to keep emotions in check to ensure a rational and productive dialogue. Emotional intelligence plays a crucial role in this process, allowing negotiators to remain calm and composed, even when discussions become tense. Recognizing the signs of escalating emotions and implementing strategies to maintain emotional equilibrium is key. This might include taking deep breaths, requesting a brief recess to collect thoughts, or employing techniques to de-escalate tension. By managing emotions effectively, negotiators can maintain a clear focus on the objectives of the negotiation, facilitating a more constructive and amicable resolution.

Communicate Clearly and Assertively: Effective communication is the cornerstone of successful negotiation. It involves expressing your needs, concerns, and proposals in a manner that is both clear and assertive, ensuring that your position is understood without resorting to aggression or passivity. Utilizing "I" statements can be a powerful way to convey your perspective in a way that is direct yet non-confrontational. For example, saying "I feel that this solution meets our mutual needs" rather than "You need to accept this" can foster a more collaborative atmosphere. Being specific and avoiding ambiguous language helps to clarify expectations and reduce misunderstandings. This clear and assertive communication style promotes transparency and understanding, making it easier to navigate the negotiation towards a successful conclusion.

Ethical Leadership

Ethical leadership is the practice of being honest, fair, and respectful in all decisions and interactions, with a commitment to doing what is right. It involves leading with integrity and responsibility, ensuring that ethical principles guide one's actions and the organization's culture.

Ethical leadership is critical for several reasons. It builds trust among team members, stakeholders, and the broader community, fostering a positive organizational culture and reputation. Ethical leaders inspire others to uphold high standards of integrity, contributing to a more just and accountable society. Moreover, ethical leadership is essential for sustainable success, as it encourages long-term thinking and responsibility towards all stakeholders, including the environment and future generations.

Characteristics of Ethical Leaders

Ethical leaders share several key characteristics, including:

Integrity: Integrity is the bedrock of ethical leadership. Leaders who demonstrate integrity are characterized by their honesty and transparency, consistently making decisions that align with moral and ethical principles. This commitment to doing what is right, rather than what is convenient or personally beneficial, earns them the respect and trust of their team members and stakeholders. Integrity in leadership involves a steadfast adherence to a set of core values and principles, guiding actions and decisions across all situations. Such leaders serve as role models, inspiring their teams to uphold similar values in their work and interactions.

Fairness: Fair leaders are committed to treating all individuals with respect and equity, ensuring that decisions are made based on merit and without bias, favoritism, or prejudice. This commitment to fairness is crucial for building a culture of trust and respect within the team or organization. Fairness in leadership means actively recognizing and eliminating biases, providing equal opportunities for growth and development, and ensuring that all voices are heard and considered in decision-making processes. By prioritizing fairness, leaders can cultivate a more inclusive and equitable environment that values diversity and promotes collaboration.

Empathy: Empathy in leadership is about showing genuine concern and understanding for the well-being of others. Empathetic leaders are attuned to the feelings, thoughts, and experiences of their team members and stakeholders, considering the impact of their decisions on all involved parties. This quality enables leaders to connect with others on a deeper level, fostering a supportive and compassionate work environment. Empathetic leadership involves listening actively, showing compassion, and taking proactive steps to address the needs and concerns of others. By leading with empathy, leaders can enhance team cohesion, morale, and overall organizational well-being.

Accountability: Accountable leaders take full responsibility for their actions and the outcomes of their decisions, including acknowledging mistakes and implementing corrective measures when necessary. This sense of accountability is essential for fostering a culture of trust and integrity within an organization. By owning their decisions and their consequences, leaders set a powerful example for their teams, encouraging a similar sense of responsibility and ownership at all levels. Accountability in leadership also involves providing clear expectations, offering constructive feedback, and supporting team members in their efforts to achieve shared goals.

Courage: Courageous leaders possess the strength to make difficult decisions and stand up for what is right, even when faced with opposition, uncertainty, or risk. This quality is critical for navigating the challenges and ethical dilemmas that leaders often encounter. Courage in leadership means being willing to take calculated risks, challenge the status quo when necessary, and advocate for change to uphold ethical principles and achieve the greater good. By demonstrating courage, leaders inspire their teams to embrace change, face challenges head-on, and strive for excellence in their endeavors.

Strategies for Promoting Ethical Leadership

Set Clear Ethical Standards: The foundation of an ethical organization is the establishment and communication of clear ethical standards. This involves defining the values and principles that guide the organization and ensuring these are reflected in every aspect of its operations, from policies and procedures to daily interactions. Developing a comprehensive code of ethics is a critical step in this process. This code should outline the expected behaviors and decision-making guidelines that align with the organization's core values. To ensure that these standards are not just words on paper, it's essential to provide ongoing training and resources that help employees understand and apply these principles in their work. Such efforts help to create a shared understanding of what is expected, guiding employees in making decisions that reflect the organization's commitment to ethical conduct.

Encourage Open Dialogue: Creating a culture where team members feel comfortable discussing ethical concerns and dilemmas is essential for maintaining transparency and accountability. This requires fostering an environment where open dialogue is encouraged and supported. Leaders can facilitate this by holding regular meetings focused on ethical discussions, allowing employees to share their experiences, voice concerns, and seek advice on ethical matters. Such forums not only promote a culture of openness but also help to identify potential ethical issues before they escalate. Encouraging open dialogue demonstrates the organization's commitment to ethics and provides a mechanism for continuous learning and improvement.

Reward Ethical Behavior: Acknowledging and rewarding ethical behavior is a powerful way to reinforce the value placed on integrity and ethical conduct within the organization. Recognition programs that celebrate employees who demonstrate exemplary ethical behavior serve as a clear signal to all team members that ethical actions are noticed and valued. Incorporating ethical behavior as a key criterion in performance evaluations further embeds ethics into the fabric of the organization. By recognizing and rewarding integrity, organizations can inspire others to uphold the highest standards of ethical conduct, creating a positive feedback loop that encourages continuous ethical behavior.

Address Unethical Behavior Promptly: Dealing with unethical behavior swiftly and effectively is critical for upholding ethical standards. Ethical leaders must ensure that there are clear, accessible procedures for reporting unethical conduct and that these reports are taken seriously. The process for addressing unethical behavior should be fair, consistent, and transparent, ensuring that all actions taken are in line with the organization's ethical guidelines. Promptly addressing unethical behavior not only rectifies immediate issues but also serves as a deterrent for future misconduct. It reinforces the message that unethical actions will not be tolerated, helping to maintain trust and integrity within the organization.

Chapter Eight: Time Management and Productivity

Effective time management is essential for achieving goals, reducing stress, and enhancing productivity. At the heart of time management lies the ability to prioritize tasks efficiently—distinguishing between what is urgent and what is important, and allocating resources accordingly. Task prioritization involves evaluating a list of tasks and determining the order in which they should be tackled based on their relative importance and urgency. This process ensures that critical, high-impact activities are completed before less critical ones, optimizing productivity and ensuring progress towards goals.

Prioritizing Tasks

The Eisenhower Matrix: The Eisenhower Matrix is a powerful tool for organizing tasks based on their urgency and importance, aiding in prioritization and decision-making. By categorizing tasks into four quadrants—Urgent and Important, Important but Not Urgent, Urgent but Not Important, and Neither Urgent nor Important—you can clearly see where to focus your attention and energy.

- **Urgent and Important tasks** demand immediate attention and are critical for achieving your goals. These should be your top priority.

- **Important but Not Urgent tasks** are essential for long-term success and should be scheduled into your routine to prevent them from becoming urgent.

- **Urgent but Not Important tasks** can often be delegated to others, as they require immediate attention but do not significantly contribute to your overall objectives.

- **Neither Urgent nor Important tasks** are the least critical and should be minimized or eliminated altogether to free up time for more valuable activities.

To utilize the Eisenhower Matrix effectively, regularly list and assess your tasks, assigning them to the appropriate quadrant. This will help you to focus on tasks that are truly critical and manage your time more efficiently.

The Pareto Principle (80/20 Rule): The Pareto Principle, or the 80/20 Rule, posits that a small proportion of your efforts (approximately 20%) typically accounts for a large portion (around 80%) of your results. This principle encourages you to identify and concentrate on the tasks that yield the most significant impact.

- To apply the Pareto Principle, start by analyzing your tasks and identifying which ones contribute the most to achieving your goals. Look for patterns in your work where a small amount of input leads to substantial outcomes.

- Once you've identified these high-impact tasks, prioritize them in your schedule, dedicating more resources and energy to these areas. This might involve reallocating time from less productive activities or streamlining processes to focus more on these key tasks.

Time Blocking: Time blocking is a technique that involves dividing your day into blocks of time, each dedicated to accomplishing a specific task or group of tasks. This method is particularly effective because it allows you to focus deeply on one task at a time, minimizing distractions and ensuring that priority tasks receive the attention they need.

- To implement time blocking, start by identifying the times of day when you are most productive and alert. Schedule your most important and demanding tasks during these peak periods to take advantage of your natural energy levels.

- Allocate specific time blocks for these tasks, making sure to include clear start and end times. Be realistic about how much time each task will require and avoid overloading your schedule.

- Incorporate short breaks between time blocks to rest and recharge, which is essential for maintaining high levels of focus and productivity throughout the day.

- Adjust your time blocks as needed based on task completion and any unforeseen demands on your time.

The ABCDE Method: The ABCDE Method is a prioritization technique that helps you categorize tasks based on their importance and urgency. This method ensures that you focus on your most critical tasks first, improving efficiency and effectiveness.

- Begin by listing all the tasks you need to accomplish. Then, categorize each task using the ABCDE method, where 'A' tasks are most important and urgent, 'B' tasks are important but less urgent, 'C' tasks are nice to do but not as critical, 'D' tasks can be delegated to someone else, and 'E' tasks can be eliminated from your schedule.

- Prioritize completing 'A' tasks before moving on to 'B' and 'C' tasks. This ensures that your most important work is completed first, reducing stress and increasing your sense of accomplishment.

- Regularly review and adjust your task categories as priorities shift, ensuring that your focus remains on the most impactful activities.

Reflection and Adjustment: Regular reflection on your time management and prioritization strategies is crucial for continuous improvement. By assessing what is working well and what could be improved, you can make informed adjustments to your approach.

- At the end of each day or week, take some time to review the tasks you completed and evaluate how effectively you prioritized and managed your time.

- Consider what strategies helped you be productive and identify any areas where your approach could be refined. For example, if you find that certain tasks took longer than expected, you may need to allocate more time in your schedule for similar tasks in the future.

- Based on this reflection, make necessary adjustments to your time management strategies, experimenting with different techniques to find what works best for you.

Overcoming Procrastination: Techniques for Staying Motivated

Procrastination, the act of delaying or postponing tasks, is a common barrier to productivity that many individuals face. It can stem from various psychological factors, including fear of failure, perfectionism, or lack of motivation. Overcoming procrastination involves understanding its root causes and implementing strategies to stay motivated and focused on your goals.

Procrastination is not merely a time management issue but often a complex emotional and psychological challenge. It can be a coping mechanism for dealing with anxiety associated with a task or an avoidance behavior driven by an aversion to the task itself. Recognizing the underlying reasons for procrastination is the first step toward overcoming it.

Techniques for Overcoming Procrastination

Break Tasks into Smaller Steps: Large or complex tasks can often seem daunting, which can lead to procrastination. By breaking these tasks down into smaller, more manageable steps, they become less intimidating and more approachable. This method not only simplifies the task but also provides a clear roadmap for completion.

- Start by identifying the overall goal or final outcome of the task. Then, divide the task into smaller segments or actions that lead toward this goal. Each step should be actionable and specific enough to focus on without feeling overwhelmed.

- Begin with the first step, concentrating solely on completing that piece before moving on to the next. This focused approach helps maintain attention and reduces anxiety about the task's overall scope.

- Celebrate the completion of each step, no matter how small. This sense of achievement can build momentum and motivate you to continue progressing through the task.

Set Clear Deadlines: Deadlines are powerful motivators that can help combat procrastination by creating a sense of urgency. Without a deadline, it's easy to keep pushing tasks off into the future.

- For each task or step within a larger project, establish a specific, realistic deadline. Consider the time required to complete the task comfortably without rushing, but also without allowing too much leeway for procrastination.

- Use tools such as calendars, planners, or digital reminders to keep track of these deadlines. Setting alarms or notifications a few days before a deadline can help ensure that you remain aware of upcoming due dates.

- If a task does not have an external deadline, create one for yourself and treat it with the same seriousness as you would a deadline set by someone else. Share your self-imposed deadlines with a colleague or friend if external accountability helps you stay on track.

Use Positive Reinforcement: Positive reinforcement is a technique that involves rewarding yourself for completing tasks or making progress, which can increase motivation and reduce the tendency to procrastinate.

- Develop a reward system for yourself, where you earn a specific reward for completing a task or reaching a milestone. Rewards should be meaningful and enjoyable, providing genuine motivation to complete the work.

- Rewards can vary depending on personal preferences and the nature of the task. It could be something as simple as taking a short break to do something you enjoy, having a snack, or engaging in a favorite hobby.

- It's important to only grant the reward after the task or step is completed. This conditions your brain to associate the completion of tasks with positive outcomes, making it more likely that you'll tackle tasks promptly in the future.

Eliminate Distractions: Distractions can significantly impede your ability to focus and complete tasks efficiently, serving as one of the primary drivers of procrastination. Creating a work environment that minimizes distractions is crucial for maintaining concentration and productivity.

- Start by identifying the sources of distraction that most often disrupt your work. Common culprits include social media, email notifications, noisy environments, or even personal concerns that occupy your thoughts.

- Implement measures to reduce these distractions. This might involve using apps or tools designed to block access to distracting websites or social media during work hours. Turning off notifications on your phone or computer can also help minimize interruptions.

- Choose a workspace that supports focused work. If noise is a distraction, consider using noise-cancelling headphones or seeking out a quiet location. Tailoring your work environment to facilitate concentration can make a significant difference in your ability to stay on task.

Change Your Environment: A change in your work environment can stimulate your senses and provide a new perspective, often leading to increased motivation and productivity. Different settings can inspire different levels of creativity and focus.

- If you're feeling stuck or unmotivated, consider changing your physical location. This could be as simple as moving to a different room in your home or office, or as refreshing as working from a café or public library for a few hours.

- Even small changes in your immediate workspace can have a positive impact. Try reorganizing your desk, adding some plants or artwork, or adjusting the lighting to create a more pleasant and stimulating environment.

- Experiment with different environments to find the settings that work best for you. Some people thrive in the quiet solitude of a home office, while others find energy in the bustling atmosphere of a coffee shop.

Practice Self-Compassion: Harsh self-criticism for procrastinating can lead to a cycle of guilt and avoidance, making it even harder to get back on track. Practicing self-compassion is key to breaking this cycle and fostering a healthier approach to work and productivity.

- When you notice you're being overly critical of yourself for procrastinating, take a moment to practice self-compassion. Acknowledge that procrastination is a common experience and doesn't reflect your worth or capabilities.

- Speak to yourself as you would to a friend in the same situation. Offer words of encouragement and understanding, recognizing that setbacks are a natural part of the learning and growth process.

- Gently guide yourself back to the task at hand, focusing on small, manageable steps you can take to make progress. Celebrate the effort, not just the outcome, and recognize that moving forward, no matter how slowly, is a positive step.

Productivity Tools and Techniques: Maximizing Efficiency

In the quest for peak performance in both personal and professional spheres, leveraging productivity tools and techniques is essential. These tools and methodologies can significantly enhance efficiency, helping individuals manage their time effectively, streamline workflows, and achieve more with less effort.

Productivity tools and techniques are designed to facilitate task management, organization, and prioritization, enabling individuals to focus on their most important tasks. From digital applications to time-tested methodologies, the right tools can transform the way you work and live.

Task Management Apps: Digital task managers are incredibly valuable for keeping track of tasks, deadlines, and projects. By breaking down larger projects into more manageable tasks and setting priorities, these apps help ensure that you stay on track and meet your objectives. The ability to synchronize your task list across devices means that your to-do list is always at your fingertips, whether you're at your desk or on the go.

- When choosing a task management app, consider the features that are most important to you, such as ease of use, customization options, and integration with other tools you use. Once you've selected an app, commit to using it consistently as the central hub for all your tasks and projects.

- Utilize the app's features to organize your tasks by project or category, set deadlines, and prioritize your work based on urgency and importance. Regularly updating your task list and tracking your progress can help keep you motivated and on track.

Calendar Apps: Digital calendars are essential for managing your time and ensuring that you allocate your day effectively. They allow you to schedule appointments, set reminders, and block off time for focused work sessions and breaks.

- Use your digital calendar to plan your week in advance, scheduling time for both fixed commitments like meetings and flexible time blocks for completing tasks. This helps to ensure that you have a clear plan for how to use your time each day.

- Color-coding different types of activities can make your calendar more visually organized and make it easier to see at a glance how your time is allocated. For example, you might use one color for meetings, another for deep work sessions, and a third for personal time.

Note-Taking Apps: Note-taking apps are indispensable for capturing ideas, storing information, and organizing your thoughts. With features like tagging and search capabilities, these apps make it easy to keep your notes organized and accessible.

- Develop a consistent system for organizing your notes that works for you. This might involve creating separate notebooks for different projects or subjects and using tags to categorize notes for easy retrieval.

- Make it a habit to regularly review and update your notes to ensure they remain relevant and useful. This can also be a good opportunity to consolidate notes and eliminate any that are no longer needed.

Time Tracking Tools: Time tracking tools provide valuable insights into how you spend your day, helping you identify areas where you can improve your efficiency. By understanding your time usage patterns, you can make informed decisions about how to optimize your workflow and eliminate time-wasting activities.

- Implement time tracking tools to monitor the duration of various tasks and activities throughout your day. This data can reveal how much time you're spending on productive work versus distractions.

- Analyze the data collected by your time tracking tool to identify patterns and areas for improvement. For example, you might discover that you're most productive in the mornings and can schedule your most important tasks during this time.

Effective Productivity Techniques

The Pomodoro Technique: The Pomodoro Technique is a time management method that breaks work into intervals, traditionally 25 minutes in length, separated by short breaks. This approach is designed to maximize focus and efficiency while minimizing the risk of burnout. By working in short, focused bursts, individuals can maintain high levels of concentration and make significant progress on their tasks.

- To implement the Pomodoro Technique, choose a task you want to work on and set a timer for 25 minutes. Commit to working on the task with full focus during this interval, avoiding all distractions.

- When the timer goes off, take a 5-minute break to rest and recharge. This short break is crucial for maintaining mental freshness and preventing fatigue.

- After completing four Pomodoro sessions (or "Pomodoros"), take a longer break of 15-30 minutes to allow for a more substantial mental recovery before starting the next cycle.

- The Pomodoro Technique can be particularly effective for large or daunting tasks, as it breaks the work into manageable chunks and provides regular breaks to keep your mind sharp.

The Two-Minute Rule: The Two-Minute Rule is a simple yet effective strategy for managing small tasks efficiently. The principle is that if a task can be completed in two minutes or less, it should be done immediately, rather than postponed. This approach helps to keep small tasks from accumulating and becoming a source of clutter and stress.

- Implement the Two-Minute Rule by immediately addressing any task that comes your way if it can be completed quickly, such as responding to an email, filing a document, or making a brief phone call.

- Applying this rule throughout your day can significantly reduce the number of minor tasks on your to-do list, freeing up time and mental energy for more significant projects.

- The Two-Minute Rule also encourages a proactive approach to task management, preventing procrastination and improving overall productivity.

Work-Life Balance: Managing Personal and Professional Life

Work-life balance involves allocating one's time and energy between work and other important aspects of life, such as family, leisure, and personal interests. It's not about equally dividing the hours of the day between work and personal life but rather about having the flexibility to get things done in your professional life while still having time and energy to enjoy your personal life. Achieving a healthy work-life balance is crucial for maintaining well-being, reducing stress, and ensuring long-term productivity and satisfaction in both personal and professional spheres.

Achieving Work-Life Balance

Set Clear Boundaries: The integration of work and personal life, especially in remote or flexible work arrangements, can lead to work encroaching on personal time. Establishing clear boundaries is essential to prevent this overlap and ensure that time off truly allows for relaxation and personal activities.

- Determine specific work hours based on your job requirements and personal preferences. Communicate these hours to colleagues and adhere to them as consistently as possible.

- Develop rituals that signal the end of the workday, such as shutting down your computer, turning off notifications, or having a specific end-of-day routine. These signals can help transition your mind from work mode to personal time.

- Be disciplined about not checking work emails or messages outside of your defined work hours, reinforcing the boundary between work and personal life.

Prioritize Your Health: Maintaining physical and mental health is foundational to sustaining productivity and enjoying your personal life. Neglecting health can lead to burnout, decreased productivity, and reduced quality of life.

- Make regular physical activity a part of your daily routine. Even short periods of exercise can have significant health benefits and improve mood.

- Pay attention to nutrition by choosing balanced meals that fuel your body and mind. Adequate hydration is also vital for maintaining energy levels.

- Ensure you get enough sleep each night, as sleep is crucial for recovery, cognitive function, and overall health.

- Incorporate stress-reduction practices such as meditation, yoga, or deep-breathing exercises into your routine to manage stress and support mental health.

Learn to Say No: The ability to decline additional commitments is critical for managing your time and energy. Overcommitting can lead to stress, burnout, and a negative impact on work quality and personal life satisfaction.

- Before accepting new commitments, evaluate them against your existing responsibilities and personal goals. Consider whether the new commitment supports your priorities or detracts from them.

- Practice saying no in a polite but firm manner. Remember, declining a request allows you to dedicate your energy to commitments you've already made and to your personal priorities.

Leverage Flexibility: Flexible work arrangements can significantly enhance work-life balance by allowing you to work in ways that best fit your lifestyle and responsibilities.

- If your job allows for flexibility, discuss options with your employer that could support a better balance, such as remote work, flexible start and end times, or a compressed workweek.

- Use the flexibility to manage personal responsibilities more effectively, such as scheduling appointments or family time during less traditional hours, provided it doesn't interfere with your work responsibilities.

- Remember, flexibility should enhance your productivity and work-life balance, not lead to longer work hours or reduced personal time.

Delegate and Outsource: Taking on all responsibilities yourself, both professionally and personally, can quickly lead to burnout. Learning to delegate tasks effectively at work and considering outsourcing at home can significantly reduce your workload, allowing you to focus on priorities and activities that require your personal attention and expertise.

- At work, identify tasks that can be delegated to team members or colleagues. Consider each person's skills and workload before delegating to ensure the task is appropriate for them. Providing clear instructions and support as needed can help the process go smoothly.

- At home, evaluate which chores or errands can be outsourced or shared among family members. Services like grocery delivery, house cleaning, or even hiring a virtual assistant for administrative tasks can free up valuable time.

- Remember, delegating and outsourcing are not about shirking responsibilities but about managing your energy and time more efficiently.

Make Time for What Matters: With the demands of work often encroaching on personal time, it's vital to proactively schedule time for activities and people that bring joy and relaxation into your life.

- Actively block off time in your calendar for non-work activities, treating these blocks with the same level of commitment as you would a work meeting. This could include time spent with family and friends, pursuing hobbies, or simply relaxing.

- Communicate these commitments to colleagues and family members to ensure that this time is respected and protected.

- Regularly reevaluate how you spend your time to ensure that it aligns with your priorities and values, making adjustments as necessary to maintain balance.

Unplug Regularly: Regularly disconnecting from digital devices and work communication is crucial for mental well-being, maintaining personal relationships, and fully engaging in personal activities.

- Establish specific times or zones in your home where digital devices are not allowed, such as during dinner time or in the bedroom. This can help create spaces dedicated to relaxation and quality time with loved ones.

- Set boundaries around checking work emails or messages during personal time. Communicate these boundaries to colleagues to manage expectations regarding your availability.

- Use features like "Do Not Disturb" modes on your devices during personal time to minimize distractions and make it easier to disconnect.

Chapter Nine: Networking and Relationship Building

Networking is a fundamental skill in the professional world, pivotal for career development, knowledge exchange, and opening doors to new opportunities. Effective networking is more than just collecting business cards or adding contacts on LinkedIn. It's about building genuine connections with others in your field or related fields. These relationships can provide support, advice, and opportunities for collaboration, as well as increase your visibility within your industry.

Strategies for Effective Networking

Be Genuine: The foundation of meaningful professional relationships is authenticity. People are more likely to engage in a relationship when they feel a genuine connection rather than a transactional interaction.

- **Show Interest:** Demonstrate genuine curiosity about the people you meet. Ask them about their experiences, challenges, and successes. This shows that you value their knowledge and perspective.

- **Listen Actively:** Effective communication is as much about listening as it is about speaking. Pay close attention to what others say, and respond thoughtfully. This can lead to deeper understanding and more meaningful conversations.

Offer Value: Networking should not be solely about what you can gain from others but also what you can offer. Providing value to your connections can help build trust and establish a solid foundation for the relationship.

- **Share Knowledge:** If you come across information or opportunities relevant to someone in your network, share it with them. This could be in the form of articles, research papers, or job postings.

- **Offer Support:** Be ready to lend your expertise or assistance when your contacts need it. This could mean providing feedback on a project, offering advice, or making an introduction.

Utilize Social Media: Social media platforms, particularly LinkedIn, are invaluable for networking. They provide a space to connect with industry professionals, share content, and participate in discussions.

- **Engage Regularly:** Post content that adds value to your network, comment on others' posts, and join industry-specific groups. This increases your visibility and positions you as a thought leader in your field.

- **Optimize Your Profile:** Ensure your LinkedIn profile accurately reflects your current role, skills, and accomplishments. A complete and up-to-date profile is more appealing to potential connections.

Attend Industry Events and Conferences: Physical events offer a unique opportunity to build connections in a more personal setting. They also provide a platform for learning and sharing knowledge.

- **Set Objectives:** Before attending an event, identify what you want to achieve. This could include connecting with specific individuals, gaining insights into new trends, or finding potential collaborators.

- **Follow Up:** After making new contacts, reach out with a personalized message to express your appreciation for the conversation and propose a way to stay in touch. This could be through LinkedIn, email, or even a coffee meeting.

Follow Up and Stay in Touch: Following up is a crucial step in transforming a new acquaintance into a lasting professional relationship. A personalized follow-up not only demonstrates your interest but also helps to reinforce the connection made during your initial interaction.

- **Timely Follow-Up:** Aim to send a follow-up message within 24-48 hours of your meeting. This ensures that your meeting is still fresh in both parties' minds.

- **Personalize Your Message:** Mention a specific topic or detail from your conversation. This personal touch shows that you were genuinely engaged in the interaction and helps to solidify the connection.

Cultivate a Giving Mindset: A giving mindset in networking is about focusing on how you can be of service to others, rather than what you can gain from them. This approach can lead to more fruitful and reciprocal relationships.

- **Offer Support:** Whether it's sharing relevant information, providing introductions, or offering your expertise, look for ways to assist your contacts. Doing so without expecting anything in return can lead to stronger, trust-based relationships.

- **Be a Connector:** One of the most valuable things you can do is to connect people within your network who could benefit from knowing each other. This not only helps your contacts but also establishes you as a valuable and resourceful member of your network.

Be Patient and Persistent: The process of building a strong and effective network is a marathon, not a sprint. Patience and persistence are key virtues in this endeavor.

- **Stay Engaged:** Regularly engage with your network through social media, emails, and attending events. Consistency in engagement keeps you on their radar and helps to strengthen your relationships over time.

- **Value Quality Over Quantity:** It's better to have a smaller network of strong, meaningful relationships than a large network of superficial connections. Invest time in developing these relationships.

- **Be Open to the Long Game:** Understand that not all networking efforts will yield immediate benefits. Some relationships may take time to develop into opportunities or collaborations. Stay patient and keep nurturing these connections.

Personal Branding

Personal branding is about intentionally shaping the perception others have of you, based on your strengths, skills, values, and the unique contributions you can make. It's about telling your story in a way that resonates with your professional goals and the needs of your target audience. A strong personal brand can enhance your visibility, establish your expertise, and open up new opportunities for career advancement.

Developing Your Personal Brand

Define Your Unique Value Proposition: The path to defining your unique value proposition begins with a deep introspection of what truly sets you apart from others in your professional field. This differentiation factor is not merely about your skills or experiences; it's about the amalgamation of your strengths, passions, and the distinctive value you bring to the table in your industry. To unearth this unique value proposition, start by reflecting on the feedback you've received over your career, the projects where you've not just succeeded but excelled, and the topics that ignite your passion.

Your unique value proposition is your professional signature—it's what makes you memorable in the vast sea of industry professionals. It requires you to dig deep into your professional journey, identifying those moments and achievements that truly define you. This could be a unique approach to solving problems, an innovative project you spearheaded, or an uncommon skill set that bridges diverse domains. The goal is to articulate this unique blend of attributes in a way that resonates with your audience, making it clear why you are the go-to person in your particular niche.

Establish Your Professional Goals: The foundation of a powerful personal brand is a clear understanding of your professional goals. These goals act as the guiding star for the development and evolution of your personal brand. By defining clear, achievable objectives, you anchor your personal branding efforts in purpose and direction. These goals should span the short to long term, covering immediate aspirations as well as your vision for your career's trajectory.

When setting these goals, it's crucial to be introspective about how you wish to be perceived within your industry. Ask yourself what achievements you aim for and the positions you aspire to hold. This clarity will not only help you chart a path for your career but also inform the messaging and strategies behind your personal branding efforts. Whether you aim to be recognized as a thought leader, an innovator, or a key influencer in your field, your professional goals will shape the narrative of your personal brand.

Craft Your Professional Story: Your professional story is essentially the narrative arc of your career. It's a cohesive and compelling account of your journey, achievements, and the unique value you offer. This story should be authentic, resonating with your personal brand and the audience you aim to engage. It's about connecting the dots of your professional life in a way that highlights not just your successes, but also the lessons learned and the challenges overcome.

Developing an "elevator pitch" is a critical exercise in this process. This pitch is a succinct summary of your professional story, designed to communicate the essence of who you are and what you do in a matter of seconds. It should spotlight key milestones and successes that have significantly shaped your career. This narrative is not just a recounting of your CV but a strategic articulation of your journey, designed to engage listeners and leave them wanting to learn more about you and your work.

Optimize Your Online Presence: In today's digital-centric world, your online presence is a vital component of your personal brand. This presence extends across various platforms, from social media profiles to professional websites and digital portfolios, all of which should consistently reflect your personal brand. Regularly updating your LinkedIn profile, for instance, ensures that your professional accomplishments and current roles are accurately represented.

Creating professional content that showcases your expertise is another critical aspect of optimizing your online presence. This could be through blog posts, articles, or videos that contribute valuable insights to your industry. Engaging with your professional community online further amplifies your presence and establishes you as an active participant in your field.

Ensuring consistency across all your digital platforms is key. This consistency should be evident not just in the visual elements like profile pictures and cover images but also in the tone and substance of the content you share. This coherent online presence strengthens your personal brand, making it easier for your audience to recognize and engage with you across different platforms.

Demonstrate Your Expertise: Demonstrating one's expertise is a critical element in promoting and solidifying one's personal brand. This not only establishes authority in one's field but also sets the groundwork for being recognized as a thought leader. Sharing knowledge and insights can take many forms, including speaking engagements, writing articles, and actively contributing to discussions within the field. Each of these activities serves to showcase one's depth of knowledge, analytical capabilities, and commitment to the field.

Seeking opportunities to contribute one's expertise can significantly enhance visibility and credibility. Guest blogging on reputable platforms, participating in podcasts, conducting webinars, or speaking at conferences are potent ways to reach a wider audience, share professional insights, and engage with the community. These contributions, when shared on social media channels, not only increase one's digital footprint but also invite engagement, further expanding one's network and influence.

The key to effectively demonstrating expertise lies in the consistent delivery of value through one's knowledge and insights, thereby nurturing trust and respect within the professional community. This, in turn, solidifies one's personal brand as a reliable and authoritative source in the field.

Seek Feedback and Adapt: The way to personal branding is continuous and dynamic, necessitating regular reflection, feedback, and adaptation. Seeking feedback from peers, mentors, and industry experts is invaluable for gaining insights into how one's personal brand is perceived externally. This feedback provides a mirror through which one can evaluate the effectiveness of their personal branding efforts and identify areas for improvement.

Conducting periodic personal brand audits allows for a systematic review of one's online presence, communication, and overall brand alignment. This involves assessing the consistency of the message, the relevance of the content shared, and the engagement levels with the audience. Such audits are critical for ensuring that one's personal brand remains relevant, impactful, and aligned with career aspirations.

Being open to constructive criticism and willing to make strategic adjustments based on feedback is crucial for personal brand evolution. It signifies a commitment to growth, adaptability, and continuous learning. As the professional landscape and personal goals evolve, so too must one's personal brand. This adaptive approach ensures that the personal brand remains a true reflection of one's professional identity and aspirations, capable of navigating the changing dynamics of the industry.

Afterword: Keeping Connections Alive

Long-term relationship management in a professional context is about maintaining and deepening connections beyond initial contact. It involves regular communication, mutual support, and the continuous exchange of value. The goal is to create a network of professionals who genuinely care about each other's success and can rely on each other for support, advice, and opportunities.

At the heart of any enduring relationship lies consistent communication. This concept transcends the mere frequency of interactions to emphasize the quality and thoughtfulness behind each exchange. It's not about being in constant contact, which can sometimes feel overwhelming or intrusive. Instead, it's about creating a rhythm of meaningful interactions that reinforce the bond between the individuals involved.

Implementing regular check-ins plays a crucial role in this strategy. These check-ins could take various forms, depending on the nature of the relationship and the preferences of the individuals involved. For some, a weekly email update might be the perfect way to stay connected, providing a space to share professional developments, personal news, or simply thoughts and reflections on recent events. Others might prefer the immediacy and personal touch of phone calls or video chats, offering a more direct and engaging way to catch up and provide support.

The key is to establish a communication cadence that feels natural and beneficial to both parties, ensuring that each person feels heard, valued, and connected.

Celebrate Achievements: Celebrating the achievements of your connections is a profound way to show that you value and support their success. This act of recognition not only strengthens the bond but also builds a positive and supportive environment where successes are shared and celebrated together.

Acknowledging professional milestones, such as promotions, project completions, or the achievement of a long-term goal, shows that you are genuinely invested in their success. These congratulations can be conveyed through personal messages, which add a personal touch, or through public avenues like social media, which provides broader recognition.

The act of celebrating achievements together fosters a sense of community and shared joy, reinforcing the strength and depth of your relationship. It's a reminder that you're not just observers in each other's journeys but active participants in cheering each other on towards success.

Personalize Your Interactions: By paying attention to and remembering personal details, preferences, and significant dates such as birthdays or anniversaries, you infuse warmth and genuine care into your professional relationships. This approach signals to your contacts that you see them as more than just colleagues or business connections; you recognize them as individuals with their own lives, preferences, and milestones.

Implementing a system or utilizing tools to keep track of these details is crucial for personalizing your interactions effectively. Whether it's a digital CRM (Customer Relationship Management) tool, a simple spreadsheet, or a more traditional method like a notebook, the key is to have a reliable system in place that helps you remember and act on this information. For example, sending a personalized note or gesture on a contact's birthday or work anniversary shows that you value the relationship on a personal level, not just in professional terms. This level of attentiveness can significantly strengthen the bond between you and your contacts, setting the foundation for a relationship built on mutual respect and appreciation.

Engage in Joint Ventures or Collaborations: Collaboration is a powerful catalyst for professional relationships. Engaging in joint ventures, projects, or initiatives not only builds trust but also showcases a mutual commitment to each other's success. When you work together towards a common goal, whether it's co-authoring a paper, organizing an event, or developing a project, you get to experience each other's work ethic, creativity, and problem-solving skills firsthand. This shared experience can deepen your understanding and appreciation of each other's professional capabilities and personal qualities.

Seeking out opportunities for collaboration involves being proactive and open to exploring areas of mutual interest and goals. It's about identifying synergies between your work and that of your contacts and then taking the initiative to propose collaborative projects. These collaborations can also extend your network, introducing both parties to new contacts, ideas, and opportunities, further enriching the professional relationship.

Leverage Social Media Thoughtfully: In today's digital age, social media platforms are indispensable tools for maintaining and nurturing professional relationships. They offer a space to share updates, celebrate achievements, and engage with the content of your professional network. Thoughtful engagement on social media—such as endorsing skills, commenting on updates, or sharing relevant content—can keep you connected with your contacts and aware of their professional journeys.

Regularly engaging with your connections' posts by liking, commenting, and sharing not only keeps you visible in their networks but also demonstrates your interest and support for their work. Highlighting their achievements and contributions on these platforms can further affirm the value you see in the relationship. It's about using social media not just as a broadcasting tool for your own achievements but as a platform to uplift and support those within your network.

In essence, personalizing interactions, collaborating on shared ventures, and thoughtfully leveraging social media are strategies that, when combined, significantly enhance the quality and durability of professional relationships.

These approaches demonstrate a commitment to not just maintaining but actively enriching these connections, fostering an environment of mutual respect, support, and shared success.

Best Regards,

David Cohen